THE LANDSCAPES *of* WEST SUSSEX

THE
LANDSCAPES
of WEST SUSSEX

TONY WALES

– *Photographs by* –

ROGER HOLMAN

Hilly Hoar & David Turner

Ensign
PUBLICATIONS

First published in 1994 by
Ensign Publications
2 Redcar Street,
Southampton SO15 5LL.

ISBN 185455 099 3

Publisher: *David Graves*
Jacket design: *Mark Smith*
Book design: *David Ayres*
Repro: *MRM Graphics, Winslow*
Printers: *Kyodo, Singapore*

CONTENTS

FOREWORD

I feel myself fortunate to live in Sussex, and not merely Sussex but West Sussex. Why should this be so? Perhaps only those who like me have been born and bred in the county can fully appreciate the reasons behind such a dogmatic statement, but I will do my best to explain.

Sussex has everything. A beautiful coastline (where it has not been completely spoilt by man), rolling hills which we poetically refer to as The Downs, good roads (at least in modern times), rivers, canals, railways, castles, windmills, big towns and little villages. But then all this could refer to a great many English counties. Perhaps it is the proximity to London, whilst retaining its rural atmosphere and even some of its old speech. Or is it the history going back to the Saxons who once inhabited this part of Britain.

If you are unconvinced I can only point to some of the great literary figures who have chosen to live in my own West Sussex. First and foremost the great Hilaire Belloc; poet, visionary, journalist, politician, religious figure and just plain eccentric.

Barclay Wills, who immortalised in just a very few books the South Downs and the men who dwelt and worked on them. Tickner Edwards, once a soldier and then a country cleric, who wrote more books on Sussex than most people can find nowadays. Not forgetting writers who spent some of their lives in the county. Richard Jefferies and W.H. Hudson, both of whom ended their days in West Sussex and William Blake who came to Sussex to find mental refreshment and called the village where he settled "The sweetest spot on earth".

Sussex is a fairly large English county, and it seems only appropriate that it should be divided into West and East. Not just for administrative purposes, but because the two parts are different geographically and culturally. The West is peaceful and reflective, the East much more wild and dramatic, and even the people are different in their ways and speech.

But West Sussex will speak for itself in this book, mainly through the fine photography which is the reason behind the project. My words are merely an adjunct which I hope will enhance and not detract from the marvellous pictures.

All of us who have been concerned in making this book have tried to produce something a little unusual, and not just one more Sussex book. The photographs are in many cases of less familiar views, or popular subjects seen from unfamiliar viewpoints. In my words I have tried to steer clear of guide-book prose, and to dwell on some aspects which are not always found in books of this kind. My own interest in the traditions, culture and people of West Sussex will be apparent, as well as certain personal points of view, although I have tried to be as objective as possible.

May the enthusiasm which has made this book possible, be at least in some degree, passed on to you — the reader.

Photographic credits

Roger Holman
Page number 9,10,11,13,14,15,17,19,23,25,26,27,28,29,31,32,33,35,39,43,44,45,46,47,48,49,50,51,52,53,55,58,59,60,61,62,63,64,65,66,67,68,69,71,75,79,83,85,86,87,89,90,91,92,93,94,95.

Hilly Hoar
Page number 12,22,24,37,40,41,54,56,57,72,73,74,76,77,80,81,82,84,88.

David Turner
Page number 8,16,18,20,21,30,34,36,42,70,76,77,78.

Fran Broad
Page number 38.

BOSHAM — PRONOUNCED BOSSUM

Ask a native for a place called Bos-ham and he will smile knowingly. In Saxon times it was Bosenham and for a long time now it has been Bossum, in spite of the more correct spelling. This is probably the best known village of the Chichester Harbour group, and undoubtedly one of the most important and historic places in West Sussex; quite out of proportion to its size.

Close to the cluster of fishermen's cottages, which are now in great demand by yachting enthusiasts, is the charming Quay Meadow, adjacent to the water's edge. The nearby roadway is flooded at high tides, as some car owners have discovered too late.

Bosham was a fishing village in days gone by, with some forty oyster smacks working from here in the 1800s. Today, privately owned leisure boats are everywhere, and the village is thronged with happy visitors during the sunny summer months. Somehow the little place manages to accommodate them all, and at the same time retain its ancient dignity and charm. Even Tennyson held it in regard when he made Becket say "Better have been a fisherman at Bosham".

The Venerable Bede records that even before St. Wilfrid brought Christianity to Sussex, a monk named Dicul had a small Monastery here housing half a dozen brothers, and with its own chapel. The present church dedicated to the Holy Trinity is simple without, and wonderful within. The tower and chancel are pre-Conquest, and there are many great things to be seen and enjoyed.

History is everywhere. The church is believed to be on the site of a Roman temple, and a huge marble head was dug up in the church-yard, which was assumed to be from a Saxon idol. Harold sailed from here in 1064 on his ill-fated voyage, and little Bosham appears on the Bayeux Tapestry.

Sometimes tradition takes over from history. The Danes are said to have stolen bells from the church, and this has given substance to one of the most persistent bell legends — and there are many — in Sussex. One of the stolen bells is said to have crashed through the deck of the pirate's ship, sinking beneath the waves into what is now known as Bell Hole. When the remaining bells are rung, the sunken one chimes in unison. When the villagers tried to rescue their sunken bell, they used a team of white oxen, but as always happens in a tale of this sort, one animal had a single black hair, so the ropes snapped and the attempt was foiled.

At the upper end of Chichester Harbour is Appledram (often spelt Apuldram). The original port has now vanished and has been replaced by Dell Quay.

Appledram Church

The magic that is Bosham

TWO HARBOUR VILLAGES

West Wittering, found in Domesday as Westrings, lies at the entrance to Chichester Harbour, behind the sand-spit known as East Head — which has changed several times over the years due to constant coastal erosion. On fine summer days and particularly on Bank Holidays, it is bustling with visitors and their cars, largely due to the excellent sandy beach.

It has been suggested that the Romans lived here and that the road from Chichester may have been their work, due to its straightness. In more recent times the smuggling fraternity certainly found the area to their liking particularly Snowhill Creek, which brought about the building of some new coastguard cottages and a watch-house.

Boats and more boats at West Itchenor

The church of St. Peter and Paul was poorly restored in 1875, but there are some good things from earlier centuries left inside. This was an area of early Christianity in Sussex, so every little village has its church, in many cases built on the site of an even earlier place of worship.

There is folklore a plenty. The fig trees here are supposed to have been planted by St. Richard, or was it Thomas a Becket? West Wittering shares with Tarring and Sompting the tradition of a bird similar to the Beccafico (figeater) of Campagna, in Italy, visiting the fig trees each year. Yet another legend says that King Ella of the Vikings lived in a house here, and there is supposed to have been an underground tunnel from the church to this house — which perhaps brings us back to the smugglers. West Wittering once had its own band of Christmas Mummers who performed their death and resurrection play annually in local houses and hostelries.

There are eleven square miles of tidal water in Chichester Harbour, with over a dozen interesting villages within this area. Another small port is West Itchenor — the name is said to have originated from the Saxon Icca who settled here with his people.

The village sits neatly on the harbour-side at the end of a road, lined with mainly restored 18th century houses. The original hamlet probably clustered around the church of St. Nicholas, who was appropriately the guardian of seamen. It is a simple stone edifice from the 13th century, with a new gallery inside erected in 1964. A much earlier gallery which disappeared in the 1870s was said to have been large enough to hold fifty children.

In the early 1600s Itchenor was a hive of shipbuilding activity. By the late 1700s the estate was purchased by the Duke of Richmond, who undertook a lot of building, in fact his own boat Goodwood was built here.

By the 1800s it was no longer a shipbuilding village, although this industry has been revived in a much smaller way in modern times.

Itchenor is the Customs Clearance Port for Chichester Harbour and the Harbour Conservancy has its offices in a house built on the foundations of the old village pub The Schooner.

Bathing Huts on Wittering Beach

Selsey is now a peninsula, with a causeway road leading out to the village. Once it was an island, said to be the most southerly portion of Sussex. In those days it was known as Holy Island, as according to tradition this was the spot where St. Wilfrid built his first monastery in Sussex. It was from here that he converted the heathens who had not even learnt the best way to cast nets to catch fish. When the Saint arrived, the natives were in a bad way, and it was his lesson in elementary fishing which made them listen to him when he preached the gospel of Christianity.

His original church built on a hill was dubbed The Cathedral under the Sea because it was eventually overtaken by the encroaching waters. Erosion has always been a problem here, in fact Selsey is said to have lost half a mile of its land since Domesday.

Another church replaced the original one in the 13th century, and the chancel of this church still remains as a chapel at Church Norton, the hamlet beside Selsey Harbour. In his poem Eddi's Service from Rewards and Fairies (1910), Rudyard Kipling tells of how at Midnight on Christmas Eve, none had come to attend the first Mass of Christmas, the night being particularly stormy. But Wilfrid's priest, Eddi, was determined to celebrate the mass, saying "I dare not shut his chapel on such as care to attend". But congregation there was, in the shape on an old donkey and a farm bullock! This story is said to be based on a genuine Sussex legend, and assuredly Kipling loved Sussex folklore, and much of his work draws upon it.

In the 19th century the church of St Peter's was built in the village, utilising some of the original stones from the earlier building. Now below the sea there is an area called by the fishermen The Park. This was said to be an extensive deer park, which like St. Wilfrid's first church was covered by the waters as they steadily devoured their way into the land.

Fishing was the main occupation of the early Selsey residents. Cockles, prawns, lobsters and crabs were caught in great quantities here, and a Selsey cockle was included in the traditional "Seven good things of Sussex". Every year the fishermen held a Crabber's Day, when they took time off work to spend a few hours with their families.

There was once a strange railway which linked Chichester with Selsey, known as The Hundred of Manhood and Selsey Tramway. Some idea of the line may be gained by a comment in a 1909 newspaper that this was "The noisiest and most rickety railway in England". The seven miles of track were opened in 1897, and at one time 80,000 passengers were said to have been carried in a year. The railway ended its brief years of glory in 1935.

In the nineteenth century Selsey had its own inventor, Colin Pullinger, who was born in 1815. From his factory in the High Street he claimed to follow the trades of inventor, builder, fisherman, mechanic, bell hanger, sign painter, boat builder, clock repairer, copying clerk and much, much more, ending with that of Clerk to the Selsey Sparrow Club.

Lonely path near Church Norton

Beach at Selsey Bill

Pagham Harbour, once known as Selsey Haven or Sidlesham Harbour, has been a nature reserve since 1964. This unique area is actually the remains of the sea strait which once separated Selsey (when it was an island) from the mainland. Storms caused great changes, and all that remains of the original port is a basin known as the Lagoon. At full tide the harbour is covered in water and provides a haven for wild birds, including rare varieties.

Old maps show graphically how the outline of the harbour and its mouth have changed over the centuries. A tide mill at Sidlesham ceased to exist during World War I, although at one time coal and grain had been brought by boat to supply the mill.

For many years the area had been known as a valuable natural habitat for wildlife. The first efforts to turn it into an official nature reserve took place during the second world war, when a letter in a local paper from Trooper Michael Alford was published. The well known nature writer E.M. Venables helped to bring about a meeting of people interested and the Pagham Harbour Preservation Committee was formed. Sir Richard Gregory, editor of the magazine Nature was its first chairman. Subsequently it became a sub-committee of the Bognor Regis Natural Science Society.

By this time naturalists were worried by the threat to the wildlife in the harbour from housing and caravan sites, also boating and water sports. In 1961 Mr. B.A.E. Marr prepared a detailed report for the Sussex Naturalists Trust, which was then presented to West Sussex County Council. Happily they accepted the report and entered into an agreement with the River Board to manage 690 acres of the harbour as a nature reserve. The River Board purchased the site in 1956, and in 1978 a visitors information centre and car park was provided.

There are intriguing references in old guide books to a phenomenon known as The Hushing Well. This was quite an attraction for visitors — not really a well, but an underground spring in the gravel bed of the Lagoon.

The sound of bubbles bursting on the surface of the water was described as similar to the simmering of a great cauldron.

A story from 1588 tells of a small ship sailing from the harbour manned by local men, to help harass the Spanish Armada. The little Pagham ship successfully captured a galleon The Carthagena, which ended up in Portsmouth Harbour.

There are many tales of wreckers and smugglers from this area, culminating in six local men being hanged for the murder of excise officers in 1749.

The lonely beauty of Pagham Harbour

Nature unadorned at Pagham

Described as one of the most enchanted corners of Southern England, Dell Quay in the parish of Appledram, was once ranked as the ninth most important port in the country. Now its commercial importance has disappeared, although yachtsmen and tourists sometimes appear to make it busier than ever.

This is only a part of the important general area known as Chichester Harbour, with Thorney Island at the centre, and Hayling Island to the West. Dell Quay to the East has always been considered *the* Chichester Harbour, as until the early years of the nineteenth century it was the principle depot for landing goods. In the previous century the cargoes that passed through this port included flour, timber, malt, barley, coals, wool, wine and much more. Stone foar local building was brought in here, and going back to Roman times it is more than probable that the building materials for the Palace at Fishbourne came through this part of the harbour.

Appledram was once an important salt producing area. To collect the salt, pans of clay were constructed, into which salt water was introduced. Here it was left for several years to allow it to evaporate. It was then boiled causing the salt to form crystals. These were then left to drain and dry. It sounds a slow and tiresome process, but apparently it worked well enough.

The importance of Dell Quay may be judged by the fact that it sent several ships to fight the Spanish Armada, and when Queen Elizabeth visited Chichester she granted it special harbour rights for as far as the sound of a horn blown from the Quay could be heard.

Dell Quay is now just a charming group of boatyards and cottages, but the hamlet of Appledram of which it is part, has the Church of St. Mary, originally a chapel of ease to Bosham. From the outside it is 13th century or earlier, although the interior suffered badly from a restoration in 1877. The site of the church has been conjectured as being an ancient Saxon burial ground. On the building are several interesting examples of graffiti, including some mason's marks like yachts, and a scratched design for a slender steeple.

The Ryman family were the local landowners, and the tower which was part of their Manor House still remains. The story is that William Ryman really wanted to build a castle-like home, but was forbidden to do so. The stone for the planned building had been imported from France but as William could not build as big a house as he wished some of his stone was diverted to build the bell-tower of Chichester Cathedral. This seems feasible as it was once popularly known as Ryman's Tower.

Safe in Chichester Harbour

Country meets the water at Dell Quay

One of the City of Chichester's particular attractions is its close proximity to the Harbour, with its many attractive islets, inlets and creeks. Once full of fishermen's boats and a home for many rural industries, it is now a major pleasure yachting centre, with several local sailing clubs.

The Yacht Basin at Birdham is said to be the largest in Europe with moorings for around 900 boats. There are facilities for boat repairing, chandlers and other boating shops. Birdham which is four miles from Chichester, is reached from the main A286 road.

An enjoyable walk may be taken along the banks of the old Chichester Canal, which once formed a branch of the Arundel and Portsmouth Canal. Starting at the Canal Basin, the path leads to Hunston and then out to the Chichester Channel at Birdham. Petworth House has a lovely painting of the canal, painted by Turner.

Domesday noted two fisheries and a mill at Brideham (Birdham) and valued the manor at sixty five shillings. The old Tide Mill was built in 1768, and was once worked by two owners who each owned part of the mill. Whether they enjoyed each other's proximity, or whether they sometimes fell out, we do not know; but what we are sure about is that they had to work very unusual hours in order to fit in with the tides, which provided the motive power for their machinery.

One of the owners, James Ayles, was a salt-maker (a local industry) and he owned the larger half of the mill and lived on the premises. The other, John Reeves, lived in a nearby house, probably Mill House which was later to become the headquarters of the Birdham Yacht Club, although it was burnt down in the 1970s.

The mill ceased to grind grain in the 1930s and a small Yacht Basin was developed 100 yards away near the old lockgates of the Chichester Canal. By this time these were redundant, as the Canal itself was a financial failure almost as soon as it opened, due to the coming of the railway.

The church of St. James (originally St. Leonard) was badly restored in 1882-3. It had a door in the north wall known as a devil's door. These were found in old churches and were supposed to be left open at baptisms to allow the devil to make a quick get-away, once he discovered that he would not be allowed to retain the soul of the new-born child.

Part of the old Chichester Canal at Birdham

Yachting reflections at the Chichester Yacht Basin, Birdham

Sixty two miles from London, Chichester is the worthy county town of West Sussex, with many days or even weeks of absorbing study for the interested visitor. The city is of considerable antiquity, dating from at least Roman times. Soon after the Norman Conquest Chichester became a Cathedral City. There are four important main streets, corresponding with the points of the compass, all emanating from the great Market Cross. Much of this area has been pedestrianised, which coupled with the city's ring-road makes this a delightful place for the walker. Chichester is closely entwined with the river Lavant, which although just a harmless stream most of the time, can become a raging torrent during times of continual and heavy rain, as indeed happened in the early part of 1994.

The beautiful Market Cross is one of the few remaining edifices of this kind in Southern England. It was built about 1500 by Bishop Story, and was the focal point for the commercial life of the city for centuries, until the Market House took the place of the cross in 1807. An interesting custom was carried out on New Year's Eve in the 19th century, when as the midnight chimes rang out, a number of the townsfolk perambulated around the cross three times, joined by the city band or as many members of the band who were in a fit state to play their instruments. In 1881 two bands took part, with a good bit of rivalry. As one band played God Save the Prince of Wales, the other replied with God Save the Queen. A typical example of how such bands behaved towards each other, in the good old days.

The Norman Cathedral is much loved by residents and visitors alike. It is homely and friendly, and the townsfolk have always been encouraged to use the Cathedral and its environs as if it belonged to everyone. The spire provides a prominent point for miles around due to the flat hinterland. During most of its history the Close was used as a general thoroughfare between West and South Street. This was sometimes abused, and in 1616 Bishop Harsnett during his visitation was amazed to find an alehouse had been set up in the Close, and that "boys and hoggs doe beastly defile the walls and yards belonging to the Cathedral Church". In the 19th century a watchman was appointed for the Close and nowadays the area is generally used in a reasonable and seemly manner.

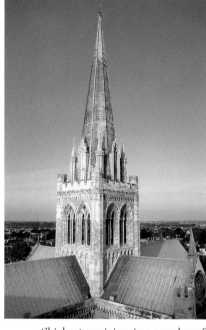

Chichester spire a landmark for miles

Chichester rejoices in a number of old traditions. It was once a happy custom to erect replica gates on the sites of the original entrances in the city walls, to celebrate royal occasions. Five of these replica gates were built for Queen Victoria's Jubilee in 1887.

The Chichester Festival Theatre was opened in 1962. It has a very unconventional design with an open stage, and before and during the building there was much opposition and pessimism over it. However the critics were proved wrong, and most now praise it without reservation.

The city was once home to many trades, not least of which was that of needlemaking. This was centred principally in the area of St. Pancras. In 1642 almost every house here was inhabited by a needlemaker. By the end of the 18th century the trade had dwindled away, due largely to competition from elsewhere offering inferior but cheaper needles. William Scale, Parish Clerk of St. Pancras was reported to be the last Chichester needlemaker.

Part of the town and
the mighty cross

A MUSEUM OF ARCHITECTURE

Singleton village, called Silletone in the Domesday survey, is a charming place full of old flint buildings, set in a valley of the Downs. It lies just about six miles from Chichester, and easily reached by bus from that city. Among its delights are the village pond, a typical Sussex village green and the church of St. John the Evangelist. This is full of good things, including stained glass and ancient graffiti.

Like so many West Sussex villages this was once a hotbed of smugglers who were said to use underground passages leading to the old Drovers Inn. On Trundle Hill, a smuggler once hung in chains after his execution following a raid in 1747. The gibbet remained until 1791 when it was said to have been struck by lightning.

The Trundle is a hill close to Singleton with many traditions attached to it. One states that a golden calf is buried here, although the Devil will not allow anyone to dig for it. Other tales tell of gold or silver treasure left by the Vikings. Anyone who tries to dig it up is prevented by a storm — or the ghost of the Golden Calf.

Many more people visit the Singleton area than would otherwise be the case, on account of the Weald and Downland Open Air Museum. This is a museum unique in Sussex, consisting of examples of vernacular country architecture. Not facsimiles, but the genuine buildings dismantled and re-erected from their original sites — but only when there is a good reason why they cannot remain there. The museum was founded by the late Roy Armstrong, who lived to see his dream become a successful reality. It opened in 1970, although the first exhibit, Winkhurst Farmhouse, was erected in 1969. Many more interesting buildings have arrived since then, most of the work being done by volunteers. One of the more recent acquisitions is an old shop from Middle Street, Horsham, which was stored in numbered pieces in the Museum for several years until it was re-erected here. On at least one occasion it has once again been used as an actual shop, staffed by a family from Horsham.

Not far away are the House, grounds and racecourse of Goodwood on the slopes of the Downs. At the turn of the century the two estates of Goodwood and West Dene totalled over 28,000 acres and even today they cover half that extent.

Racing started here in 1801, at the instigation of the 3rd Duke of Richmond, who built the first grandstand. Grand royal house parties were held at the big house in the late 19th and early 20th centuries. Goodwood Week at the end of July was of great importance to the local villages, especially Singleton. Bookmakers and horsey types descended in droves on the villages round about, with cabs travelling all the way from London. "Old Kate", a well known Cockney character, sold papers and race cards and, as one lady visitor recalled, her colourful language "lit the morning air".

The famous open air museum at Singleton

View from Goodwood looking West

KIPLING'S WHALE-BACKED DOWNS

Many writers and poets have written of the South Downs, including great literary figures like Kipling and Belloc. True-hearted Sussex folk have an especial affection for this unique natural feature, and many feel pessimistic when they watch the gradual eating away of this heritage by road builders, developers and even local authorities. We are asked to accede to the continual demand for more and faster roadways, with the unlikely excuse that it will enable the car drivers to appreciate the beauty of the downland scenery even more — presumably as they roar along at 70 miles an hour.

But all is not gloom. We can still appreciate much of the Downs, and there are even moves to bring back sheep so that the natural surface may once more gladden our footsteps. One of the finest things accomplished by the conservation bodies in recent years, has been the establishment of the South Downs Way; the whole of it in an Area of Outstanding Natural Beauty.

Of course this not an entirely new path, much of it was already in existence when the Way was officially opened by Lord Shawcross in July 1972. But the Countryside Commission designated the route as a long-distance footpath and bridle way, and thereby ensured that there were no interruptions for man (or horse) along the complete length. In fact this was the first such long distance footpath and bridle way in this country.

The route is marked with signposts at junctions and doubtful points. In West Sussex these are mostly of wood with the words South Downs Way branded into the arms, and with the symbol of an acorn. Different sections have their own individual characteristics — high and open, informal woodland or even completely enclosed by trees. Real walkers cover the whole way within a week, planning their route well ahead. But other lesser mortals may take it much more slowly or just in stages. Where it passes the summit of Bignor Hill (737 ft high), the land belongs to the National Trust, as part of the Slindon Estate. From this Hill the Way crosses the Roman Stane Street, once a very important highway.

Trotton is in the border country between Midhurst in Sussex and Petersfield in Hampshire. Trotton bridge over the Rother is a gem. It may have been built on the site of stepping stones in the bed of the river, the builder most probably being Thomas, Lord Camoys who also built the church of St. George. This is mainly from the 13th century and is famed for its brasses. The nine feet long central monument is of Thomas, his wife (Gentle) Kate and his son. In the floor is the earliest known church brass in England to show a lady. It is dated 1310 and is of Margaret de Camoys. Grooves on the church door have been explained with the romantic, and yet not entirely fanciful, supposition that they were made by Trotton men sharpening their arrows on the door before leaving for Agincourt.

Once a fashionable poet, Thomas Otway was born at Trotton in 1717. He was the son of a curate of Trotton and he died at the young age of 33, being buried in London, but with a tablet to his memory in Trotton Church. Now, not too many people will recognise his name.

Trotton Church through the tree

The South Downs Way heading East from Bignor Hill

Midhurst is a very satisfying mid-sized Sussex town. E.V. Lucas called it the most contented town in Sussex and many will appreciate his sentiment. It is an ancient borough, some say Mida or Miba of the Romans, although surprisingly not in Domesday. It was once noted for the longevity of its inhabitants, due to the pureness of the atmosphere.

The town has always been under the watchful eye of the Cowdray Estate, something which is readily apparent, if only for the mustard-yellow of the estate buildings in the area. At one time even the Estate cars and children's prams were decorated in the same colour.

The Parish Church is dedicated to Mary Magdalen and St. Denys. The first saint was probably the original dedication, with St. Denys being added later in deference to the Normans. The church has been very much restored, so not a great deal of the original building remains. All the Cowdray monuments have been removed to Easebourne church.

The very modern Roman Catholic Church of Holy Mary is in Bepton Road. Well and cleverly done in 1957, although some will find it lacking in any feel for tradition. A detached bell tower, and some interesting sculpture make this a building definitely worth visiting.

Of the several hotels and inns, "the Spread Eagle" is the best known. It is an amalgamation of buildings from the 16th, 17th and more recent centuries. Known to the locals familiarly as "The Spread", it was described by Hilaire Belloc as "that old and most revered of all the prime inns of the world", but of course Belloc considered anything from Sussex to be superior to other similar things, wherever they might be. As befits an inn of this reputation, the Spread Eagle has several ghosts; a coachman dressed in black, the Golden Lady who haunts the Edward VII room, and a young lady in Tudor costume. But local author Doris Gundry assures us that none of them are malignant.

The town is packed with old and interesting buildings. The Old Market House, which once had its ground floor open to the elements, dates from the 16th century. This was the hub of the town, with a weekly market on Thursday. The upper floor was used for meetings and under the stairs was The Cage where petty criminals were incarcerated. How the building must have looked in its heyday can be seen by visiting the Open Air Museum at Singleton and the old Market Hall from Titchfield which has been re-erected there.

Among other buildings of interest is the Old Town Hall, and the Grammar School where H.G. Wells, Cobden and Sir Charles Lyell attended as scholars.

The curfew bell was tolled here each evening at 8 o'clock. The story is that a grateful traveller who was led to the safety of Midhurst after becoming lost, gave a quarter acre of land as an endowment to pay for the nightly custom. The piece of land is known as the Curfew Garden.

Another of the town's inns The Half Moon is charmingly described by Eric Bligh in his 1968 book Two Half Moons.

Midhurst's black and white architecture

A Midhurst vicar once had the town's unemployed clearing the mud from South Pond

COWDRAY'S RUINED GRANDEUR

Cowdray took sixty years to build, but was almost completely destroyed by fire on the night of Tuesday 24th September 1793. It had been a splendid example of Tudor architecture, grand in its sober simplicity. The building was begun by Sir Davy Owen who inherited the estate in 1492. He lived at Cowdray until his death, although the estate had been bought by Sir William Fitzwilliam in 1529. Sir William who was a favourite of Henry VIII, added the Gatehouse, Tower and Hall Porch. He died in 1542, and his half-brother Sir Anthony Browne took over. He also moved within Henry VIII's charmed circle of friends and was in consequence granted Battle Abbey in 1538, which he converted for his own use.

Cowdray Castle — a window to past glories

This transaction sets the scene for the most famous curse in Sussex. When the monks were evicted from Battle Abbey, one of them cursed the new owner and prophesying that his line would perish by either fire or water. Sir Anthony Browne's considerable possessions included much taken from the treasures of the church, so it was not entirely unexpected that he should be the recipient of such a curse.

The most unusual aspect of the curse is that it took over 250 years to come into effect. It was in 1793 that the house was ravaged by fire, and its contents destroyed. The place was unoccupied at the time and the cause of the fire was thought to be a pan of charcoal left burning in the carpenter's workshop by a gang of workmen. At almost the same time, the eighth and last Lord Montague, then a young man, was drowned in an attempt to shoot the falls at Schaffhausen on the Rhine. The property then passed to Lord Montague's sister, who bore two sons and three daughters. Her husband was out boating with the boys in 1815, when the vessel overturned and the children drowned.

Cynics have often dismissed the story of the curse particularly in view of the length of time involved, although it has to be said the story has been handed on over many generations, so it is not merely a Victorian fabrication.

It was in 1533 that Sir William Fitzwilliam was licensed by the Crown to impark 600 acres and to call it Cowdray Park. The grounds were landscaped in 1770 by Capability Brown, but well before that Queen Elizabeth had sampled the delights of Cowdray, shooting several deer on one visit. Another member of the party Lady Kildare had the audacity to do likewise, much to the annoyance of Elizabeth. The Queen Elizabeth Oak in the Park purports to be the tree on which the Virgin Queen rested her bow in 1591.

Another famous visitor to Cowdray was the journalist William Cobbet who passed through in 1825 on one of his rural rides. In subsequent editions of his great work he was a little muddled over the owner of Cowdray, but he approved of the Park and remarked on the magnificent rows of Spanish chestnut trees.

The grand remains of a great Sussex house

Author Mavis Budd wrote about her grandparents who lived in the area of Stedham. She devoted three books to them and her own early days in this corner of Sussex, beginning with Dust to Dust in 1966. Her grandfather, William, was the son of Daniel Budd who was foreman at Iping Paper Mill, and her grandmother, Ellen Matilda, was the daughter of James Wells, a shoemaker who had the Post Office at Stedham. Grandfather Budd was a builder, undertaker and a country craftsman, who in his apprenticeship earned two and sixpence a week, rising a shilling a year for six years. Mr. and Mrs. Budd had a daughter, eight grandchildren and six great-grandchildren. The whole of their married life was spent in an old house going back to Elizabethan times, at the back of the workshop. An uneventful life, but one with enough commonplace interest in it to provide material for three extremely funny and wonderful books.

Life in Stedham in the past must have been fairly hard and frugal for most of the local folk, although a guide book from the beginning of the 1900s says that there was a Reading Room with a library of 150 volumes, for which villagers subscribed a penny a week. The locally-famed churchyard Yew tree was said at that time to be over 900 years old.

The village is pretty without being dramatic, with an old six arch bridge dating from the 17th century, spanning the river Rother. The extensive Common lies south of the built-up area, with Midhurst, the nearest town, to the West.

Elsted is pleasantly sited at the foot of the Downs, west of Harting. It is simple and compact, in fact E.V. Lucas in his Highways and Byways in Sussex dismissed it with the comment "Elsted has no particular interest". But of course this is not true of any village, no matter how insignificant.

The church of St. Paul like a number of such buildings in the post-Reformation period was left to decay. Then a local Lady Bountiful decided to build a very big and ugly new church at Treyford in 1849 to serve the whole area. This was called by those who liked it The Cathedral of the Downs although others were more outspoken and referred to it as The White Elephant. The church at Elsted was still used for occasional services, when a tree fell on the roof of the nave in 1893, and eventually the floor was carpeted by a good crop of grass. However the new church at Treyford itself was neglected, and it was decided to rehabilitate the old church at Elsted.

Stedham Common near to the Dust to Dust village of Mavis Budd

View across the Downs to Elsted village

ROYAL BOGNOR — JANE AUSTEN'S SANDITON

Resisting the impulse to use George V's alleged expletive on Bognor as a descriptive opening paragraph, instead I offer a more mellifluous quotation from Dally's Bognor Guide of 1828:

"The mildness of the temperature of Bognor is manifested by the luxuriance of the trees and shrubs that grow near the shore, and the facility with which all sorts of native and many exotic plants are cultivated. At the very edge of the ocean the elegant tamarisk is seen to blossom in full perfection during several of the winter months; and whilst the snow lies embedded on the northern sides of the hills, it is either not seen here, or soon dissolves away under the genial influences of the climate".

Of course this author had a vested interest, but it is impossible to deny the advantages of the climate along this part of the South coast. Unfortunately there was not too much else to claim in Bognor's favour at the time. Sir Richard Hotham energetically attempted from 1784 to turn it into a fashionable and sparkling resort, which would rival its more successful neighbours. But in spite of £60,000 of Sir Richard's money, it resolutely remained a rather unsatisfied and unfinished town.

When Sir Richard died in 1799, it was still a place in limbo — halfway between the original settlement at Bersted and the coastal fishing community. Eventually it was clear that visitors preferred the coast, and modern Bognor developed in the conventional manner of other seaside resorts from the 1820s. The pier followed those at Brighton and Worthing, in 1865, and Bognor settled down to become a pleasant and uneventful middle-of-the-road kind of South-coast town.

It had its second chance of greatness in 1929, when King George V came to Craigweil House, Aldwick, to recuperate from serious illness. But although this must have given the town much needed publicity, it appeared to make little difference to the urbane middle-class image it had adopted and Bognor continued to cater for those who preferred their seaside without too many additional distractions.

A line of sandstone rocks, which may still be discerned in the distance out to sea, were used as a lure to entice visitors; with signs on the London coaches and posters and handbills acclaiming The Rocks as if they were some kind of supernatural wonder. Those who came to look, must have pondered over what all the fuss was about, but by then they had served their purpose. Even in recent times, some residents regaled visitors with stories about buildings which they firmly maintained were once to be seen upon these rather insignificant rocks.

The beach and pier at Bognor Regis

A typical Bognor building looking seawards

UNSPOILT SLINDON

Slindon is a relatively unspoilt downland village between Chichester and Arundel. Much of it is owned by the National Trust, including many cottages, Slindon House and the Post Office.

The church of St. Mary has the only wooden effigy in Sussex. It is five feet long and is probably of St. Anthony St. Leger (1539), a knight's squire, in armour. Hilaire Belloc lived in Slindon as a child, and was much impressed by this monument; so much so that he wrote a poem which begins:

> There is no name upon his grave,
> If his grave it haps to be,
> And his face doth look toward the plain,
> And toward the calm blue sea.

One can but conjecture what lay behind the following fragment of church history; in 1782 the Rev. John Smelt, when he became Rector, agreed to pay the sum of £5 per annum for bread to the poor, replacing a feast previously given at the Parsonage.

Elizabethan Slindon House was once a Palace of the Archbishops of Canterbury. In the First World War it became a military hospital and after this a school. Earlier history mentions a secret chapel used during the days following the English Reformation.

The village, as befits such a picturesque and historic place, has many ghost stories. The best known is of a white horse which has been seen many times in Slindon Woods. It disappears as suddenly as it appears and will cause a ridden horse to stop in its tracks and refuse to move forward. Others who have not seen the ghostly horse have reported the sound of galloping hoofbeats. A local story which really ought to have a ghost attached to it, tells of the Godiva of Slindon, a country girl who fell in love with an excise man. A notorious smuggler named Ben Tapner captured Will Garland, the government official, and announced he would whip him naked across Slindon Common. Betsy offered herself in place of her lover; and so it happened, with the poor girl succumbing to her ordeal.

There are two thatched buildings in Slindon. One is a thatched railway carriage; a Stroudley 3rd Class Smoking Carriage and Guards Van, from around 1874. The other is the present-day Post Office, which was built originally as two private dwellings, the oldest part dating from the 16th century. Later it became a butcher's shop, then a greengrocers, and finally a post office in 1970.

The Nore folly, about half a mile from the village, is a flint archway which was built by the Countess of Newburgh in 1814, copying an old Italian picture. The Countess would drive out to the folly with her friends to picnic and enjoy the view. The story is that a bricklayer named Samuel Refoy who was out of work, was asked by the good lady to make a copy of her print. She was so delighted with the result that he was made the permanent estate carpenter at Slindon House.

Slindon church and God's Acre

The delightful thatched post office

PROUD PETWORTH

The old market town of Petworth is bewildering to the motorist, but entrancing for those wise enough to enjoy it on foot. In the 19th century a writer remarked that the roads were "irregular" and like most other things in Petworth, there has been little change. The town is dominated by the twelve mile long wall surrounding Petworth House and Park. Really more continental than English in its character. There are many fine buildings of all dates, and a walk around the town is a highly pleasurable experience.

The Market Place in the centre of the town is largely taken up by the solid stone building of the Leconfield Hall, where almost everything of any consequence in Petworth takes place. It was built by the Earl of Egremont in 1793 on the site of an earlier market hall which was raised on stilts.

The church dedicated to St. Mary, is a puzzle of building and rebuilding. Its earlier spire was taken down in 1800 and another (said to be intended for St. Peters, Brighton) erected in 1827. This was taken down in 1947 and in 1953 finished off with a cap. Apparently the earlier spire leant far out of the perpendicular, which gave rise to the rhyme:

Proud Petworth, poor people,

High church, crooked steeple

As we have noted the church is dedicated to the Blessed Virgin, and inside prior to the Reformation, there were two shrines to Our Lady. A short way from the town on the Fittleworth Road there still exists the Virgin Mary spring, which has a reputation for healing, especially where eye problems are concerned; so there would seem to be an obvious connection.

Petworth House was enlarged from an existing Manor House in 1309. In the sixteenth century the 8th and 9th Earls of Northumberland made further changes. The 9th Earl was known as The Wizard by reason of his alchemical experiments, which he carried out in the House. The 6th Duke of Somerset called the Proud Duke, carried out wholesale rebuilding in 1688-96. The 7th Earl left only a daughter, so the property devolved on Charles Wyndham, 2nd Lord Egremont. He was a capable and likeable man, staunchly honest at a time when many of his contemporaries were corrupt. His duties involved many banquets and he once remarked "I have but three turtle dinners to come and if I survive them I shall be immortal". He did not

survive them and was succeeded by the 3rd Earl who reigned at Petworth for 65 years.

He was a remarkable man who did a great deal for the House and the Town. Turner was a close friend and he was happy to have him living and painting in his house, treating him as an honoured guest. His eldest son was created Lord Leconfield in 1859, and in 1947 the 3rd Lord Leconfield conveyed Petworth House and grounds to the National Trust.

Worthy of mention in the history of Petworth is a wonderful local photographer, George Garland, who died in 1978. Although popular in his lifetime, his true worth as a chronicler of Petworth and Sussex social life has probably only been fully appreciated in more recent years, largely through the efforts of Petworth's Peter Jerrome and Jonathan Newdick, who have published many collections of Garland's fine photographs.

The deer in Petworth Park

*A Lilliputian-like view of
the old town of Petworth*

VILLAGE WITH A FAMOUS SHOP

Bignor's famous village shop has been round the world on picture postcards, calendars and in picture books. It is one of the most photographed shops in Sussex, although no building could be more plain or unassuming. A 15th century yeoman's cottage, half-timbered and thatched, with the first floor overhanging; and the whole incredibly unrestored. In more modern times it became a grocers shop, and it is from this period that it earned its name of The Old Shop. England was once dubbed a nation of shopkeepers and perhaps Sussex was also considered a county of shopkeepers in the minds of many, who first caught sight of its beauties by seeing a picture of this lovely unadorned building.

The Village Shop at Bignor

A further claim to fame for Bignor is the splendid Roman Villa, one of the largest in Britain. It is east of the village on the road to Bury, and was discovered in 1811 when the Bury Field was being ploughed by the young son of Mr. George Tupper, a respected local farmer. Mr. John Hawkins of Bignor Park took the subsequent excavation in hand and placed it under the supervision of a leading antiquary Samuel Lysons, and under his eye digging went on for eight years. The fine mosaic pavements found at Bignor rank in quality with any found elsewhere in the country, including Cirencester and Silchester. Experts say that the house may have lasted until the fourth or fifth century, and was then left undisturbed as it slowly fell into decay. An interesting sidelight is that in 1740 a quantity of elephant bones were dug up at Bignor, so it is possible that the Romans used elephants here.

Bignor Park was the residence of Nicholas Turner, the father of the almost-forgotten Sussex novelist and poet, Charlotte Smith, who also lived in Bignor during part of her life. She was tremendously famous in her day, and those who bought her books so voraciously then, would not have believed that she would become so little-known in future centuries.

To the east of the lovely village of Fittleworth is the expanse of Hesworth Common. In 1878 a Fittleworth lady, Charlotte Latham noted down the many superstitions and pieces of ancient lore which she found in the village and the surrounding area. She was obviously a lady of intelligence with a very keen and enquiring mind, and many of her findings concerned the natural wonders of the woods and commons around Fittleworth.

Some of these beliefs were attached to birds, particularly the magpie. Whenever villagers saw this bird on their left hand they took off their hats and bowed to it. Presumably to avert the bad luck which the magpie was said to bring with it. Another bird of ill omen to Fittleworth folk, was the raven, which was also supposed to have the power of foretelling the future. Not surprisingly, another bird disliked by the ignorant was the screech-owl. Hearing and seeing one of these birds sitting solemnly on the roof of the church, Mrs. Latham was told by a neighbour that this was a clear sign of an imminent death in the parish.

Hesworth Common near Fittleworth

OLD AND STRONG AT THE SWAN

Fittleworth, or as it was once spelt Fytelworth, is a pleasant little village three miles from Pulborough and the same distance from Petworth. There are really two Fittleworths — one with the church at the top end, and the other with the inn and river at the bottom. Here the Rother joins the Arun, a Sussex location particularly favoured by anglers.

The church is one of the many dedicated to the Virgin Mary, a recollection from the time when England was thought to be under the particular protection of the Queen of Heaven. It dates from the 13th and later centuries, with some 19th century changes which are now considered a mistake. The sturdy plain tower remains from the earlier era.

Many visitors remember Fittleworth because of The Swan, a coaching inn which started life as two 14th century cottages. Its distinctive inn sign

Fittleworth church and churchyard

which spanned the road has appeared in many paintings; in fact this was once known at The Artists pub. Many of the pictures were said to have been painted and left as payment for room and board. Poets also frequented the pub, and an unnamed one has left us these lines:

Who loves a glass of English ale,
Can get it at the Swan,
The flavour rich and colour bright,
The draught both old and strong.

The attractive creeper-covered arch has featured in some of the local tales. For instance there is one which tells of Jim Rapley, a local farmer, who promised his workers a gallon of ale if they managed to pile the hay on his cart high enough to touch the arch. The story does not tell us if they succeeded or whether he kept his word.

One of Fittleworth's worthies was George Attrill who lived there all his life, in the same cottage, with just his cats for company. He was a retired road mender, one of the useful band of man who cared for a section of a Sussex road, in the days when mechanical aids were far in the future.

George had some incredible recollections, including the Saturday night song sessions at the Swan, poaching with a gun disguised as a walking stick and of playing Father Christmas in the Fittleworth Mummers Play, or Tipteers as he called them — a role for which he needed no false beard.

Sussex has many legends of huge snakes or even dragons. Fittleworth has its own tale of a beast of this ilk which terrified the locals in the 1860s. It was described as Audaciously Large and would not allow anyone to pass its lair, without rushing out and driving back the interloper with a terrible hissing.

On a more pleasant note; Edward Elgar, lived just outside the village from 1917 to 1921, composing several of his well known works there.

A colourful view of Fittleworth Mill

In 1965 when Ian Nairn and Nikolaus Pevsner composed the Sussex volume of The Buildings of England they referred to Kirdford as "A gracious place, with almost the air of a small town". Happily this descriptive comment still applies, as those who dwell here will undoubtedly agree.

Typical of the pride with which residents view their village is the handsome handmade sign, topped with examples of glass and iron, the two major local industries of the past — although now it should be fruit and agriculture. The sign was erected in 1937 to commemorate the Coronation of King George VI, being paid for entirely by local subscription.

Although only four and a half miles from Petworth, Kirdford has always kept its larger neighbour at arm's length. It has been recorded that one local referred slightingly to Petworth as a village. Perhaps this determination to retain its own identity has something to do with the rich industrial history of the area. The abundant woodland provided ample fuel supplies for the Wealden industries of glass and iron. These reached their peak in the 16th and 17th centuries, with beech and oak being used for the many small glass furnaces.

Large quantities of charcoal were required by the itinerant glass makers who set up in one place for a time, and then moved on as the fuel was expended. The local glass was used mainly for windows and small bottles. Kirdford, Wisborough Green and Chiddingfold churches all have small windows graced with locally-made glass.

At Little Slifehurst Farm, a complete glass furnace was discovered when a drain was being dug, and in several other sites fragments of locally made glass have been found.

There were at least four Kirdford iron furnaces; the ones we know about being at Barkfold, Ebernoe, Roundwick and Shillinglee. These probably made such things as cannon balls, firebacks, kitchen pots, and pig iron for local blacksmiths.

Another unusual local industry was the quarrying of Petworth or Sussex marble. This was a freshwater limestone found in small stream valleys. It came in various shades of bluish-grey mottled with yellow, which took a high polish. Extremely popular in Sussex, examples include the font of Kirdford Church of St. John the Baptist. The floor of the church was also originally paved with the local marble but sadly this was replaced with ornamental tiles in 1878.

The village has another sign which never fails to interest visitors. The message on the sign begins with ominous words "The Degradation of Drunkenness" and goes on to point out the follies of over indulgence. Several origins are cited for the sign. One is that it was a local vicar who was being warned against his intemperate habits, although the more likely origin is that it was just one of a number of 19th century temperance plaques — although it appears to be the only one to have survived in Sussex.

*Kirdford warning
to drunkards*

*Kirdford church and
unique village sign*

ARUNDEL'S ROMANTIC BUILDINGS

Many distant views which enchant, are a disappointment when viewed from close by. Not so Arundel, where the view across the meadows to Arundel's dream-like skyline of Castle, Church and Cathedral, is more than equalled by the beauties and atmosphere of the place itself. Arundel has everything a visitor could possibly want, and even the residents seem pretty content. First there is the river Arun, once a thriving commercial waterway but now just one of the town's many attractions. Then the lovely High Street climbing uphill from the bridge and market square to the cathedral on the crown of the hill, where the Downs appear to meet the town. And over it all, not in any way menacing, but if anything benevolent and peaceful, the Castle. Not the original buildings, as only a limited amount of these remain, but a complete 19th century re-creation of a medieval castle, as imagined by the architect C.A. Buckler.

The early parts of the castle that do still exist go back to Saxon times, and there were many additions over the centuries from then onwards. Not surprisingly there are many legends entwined with the material remains. The best known concerns Arundel's own hero, Sir Bevis, the giant son of Sir Guy of Southampton and a Scottish Princess. His size was so great that he could stride across the Solent to the Isle of Wight just for a morning excursion. He first became the warden of the castle, when he offered his services to the Earl in return for an ox, a Southdown sheep, two barrels of ale and as much bread and mustard as he liked. He had a mighty horse, a great staff, and a famous sword called Morglay or Mongley. On his 100th birthday he flung this sword as far as he could and it landed in Arundel Park. At this spot he was buried and it is now known as Bevis's Grave.

Swanbourne Lake within the Park is a dream of loveliness on a summer's day. An old historian described it thus "Perhaps of all the beautiful spots in the neighbourhood of Arundel, none comprises more real beauty than this. The valley in front, shaded by the willows and ash, which adorn the little islands of the lake, and winding its way in the distance amongst the hills; the castle projecting boldly from the eminence on the left, and seeming as if suspended between earth and heaven".

The lake rises from springs at its south-east extremity, and ultimately feeds into the river Arun. The ancient mill, immortalised by Constable, no longer stands, but is recalled by the name Mill Road which leads to the lake; a charming road flanked by noble trees, although now it is often choked with cars on a fine Sunday. Beside the lake, the Arundel family, the Harbers, who were old style charcoal burners, once had their humble dwelling and kiln.

The beautiful Swanbourne Lake in Arundel Park

Arundel Castle serenely watches over the old town

THE CATHEDRAL THAT CHANGED ITS NAME

Arundel's Roman Catholic Cathedral was originally just a church, albeit as we can see, an important and imposing one. It was built in the 1870s and paid for by the fifteenth Duke of Norfolk to celebrate his coming of age. Its magnificence typified the new spirit of optimism felt by English Roman Catholics, when the dark days emanating originally from the English Reformation were at last coming to an end. The design in French Gothic was by J.A. Hansom, who is perhaps better remembered for designing Sherlock Holmes' favoured mode of transport, the Hansom Cab. As in the case of the 19th century castle buildings, the architectural establishment had some serious misgivings about the design, but time has proved that most other folk are very happy with both. At the time of building there were serious problems over the foundations, and some of these had to be sunk to a depth of 57 feet. In modern times these problems have reappeared.

When it was opened in July 1873, the dedication was to St. Philip Neri; later this was changed to Our Lady and St. Philip, and ultimately when the new Diocese of Arundel and Brighton was created, it became the Cathedral of Our Lady and St. Philip Howard. This St. Philip was the 13th Earl of Arundel, one of the English Roman Catholic Martyrs. In 1971 his remains were transferred from the Fitzalen Chapel in the Castle to the Cathedral.

Perhaps some may feel a tinge of regret towards the original St. Philip Neri, although he still has his own special altar within the Cathedral. The interior of the building is in no way a disappointment after the grandeur of the outside. The inside is light with a strong feeling of space and colour — not at all as sombre as many other similar religious buildings. The side altars are worth more than a cursory glance, and there are many other features to make a lengthy visit almost obligatory. The liturgical changes which followed the Second Vatican Council separated the main altar from its original site, and it now stands isolated in the middle of the Sanctuary.

The river Arun was once of tremendous importance to Arundel in the days when the town was a busy port. The history of this river activity goes back a long way, and it is recorded that a quantity of Caen stone was imported by water to Arundel in 1066. In 1817 it became a Bonding Port, and even up to the 1920s the whistle of the tug boat Jumna brought excited locals down to the river side.

The river was known for its mullet, a fish long regarded as a delicacy — Arundel folk who had been born in the town still consider they have a right to be termed Arundel Mullets.

The river Arun and modern waterside buildings at Arundel

The very un-English outlines of Arundel's Cathedral

THE VILLAGE LOVED BY ITS VICAR

Burpham is one of the loveliest of the Downland villages, about three miles from its big neighbour Arundel, and half way through the Arun gap. It is spread over several hillocks, at the end of a cul-de-sac; which by car, is a good deal easier to enter than to leave.

The church of St. Mary is a gem, dating from the 12th and 13th centuries, with sympathetic additions in the 19th. There is a leper's window, and a leper's path across Perry Hill.

An earth rampart was, according to tradition, built by the Saxons against Danish pirates. Here there is a Jacob's Ladder known locally as The Seventy Steps. The story always told is that this was used by the smugglers, who came up the Arun to the pub with their illicit spirits and 'bacca.

The village with its wealth of flint and brick buildings, is blessed with history and folklore disproportionate to its size. The best known local legend concerns Jack Upperton, who was hanged in 1771 on the very spot where he held up the Royal Mail in 1770. On the evening of September 26th, Jack a poor labourer and another unnamed man, held up the post boy on his way to Steyning. It was the custom at this time to use post boys as they were considered lighter, faster and obviously cheaper. Boys as young as 12 years old were employed, and there were severe penalties for those who delayed or otherwise interfered with the letters.

Although there were certainly two people involved in the robbery, the second man was never found and many believed that Jack 'covered up' for his accomplice. He is said to have told the vicar who visited him in prison "It was a "scrambling" sort of turn-out..." — the word scrambling was used in Sussex to mean mixed-up. Jack was sentenced to death at East Grinstead on March 18th 1771, and his body was to be hung in chains on Burpham New Down, close to where the crime had been committed. The blacksmith who made the gibbet was apparently paid £5 for the job.

By 1850 the gibbet had completely disappeared but was replaced by another, and the spot was later marked by a plaque inscribed J. U. 1771. This eventually disappeared but was replaced by another. Now the spot is once again difficult to find.

The Rev. Edward Tickner Edwards was the vicar who loved Burpham so much that he returned to the village in 1927 after living there as a young man. He became its vicar in that year and remained in the place until he died in 1945 and was buried in its churchyard. Without doubt he was held in high regard by his flock, but it is for his prodigious output of books about Sussex and the countryside that he is remembered by many more. In 1911 he published the book Neighbourhood, which was an account of a year's life in an English village which he called Windlecome, although most will agree the description sounds very much like his beloved Burpham. As a writer Tickner Edward has been compared to those two famous country writers Hudson and Jefferies, although his works never sold in quite the same quantities as these two. The Lore of the Honey Bee (1908) has become a classic of its kind and one of his novels, Tansy which he wrote in 1914 was later made into a film and shown in over 16,000 cinemas. Now his works are much sought after by collectors; so much so that his novels have become almost impossible to find.

Houses in beautiful Burpham

Village and church of St. Mary, Burpham

Although virtually only one long street and without any imposing buildings apart from the Castle and Church, Amberley is one of the show villages of West Sussex. It has been called the Pearl of Sussex, the loveliest village in Sussex, and the Artist's Village. The houses make up a complete catalogue of Sussex building materials — thatch, tile, brick, flint, timber and stone.

As if this was not enough, there is the imposing sight of the Castle, which commands a view of the valley through which the river Arun flows. This was an Episcopal residence from Norman times, although it was not until 1377 that Bishop Rede was granted a license to crenelate, and it took on the appearance of a castle. In spite of that it was hardly worthy of the title, being a Manor House during most of its life. It was plundered in 1643 after the surrender of Arundel Castle, but otherwise it has led a very peaceful existence. Now it is a fine country hotel.

Amberley has long been beloved of artists and craftsmen. The most famous of the former to make his home here was Edward Stott, born in

Rochdale in 1859; He came to Amberley in 1885 and grew to love it. He remained in the village until he died in 1918, providing a figure of affection for the villagers who were tolerant of his many eccentricities. He was a great walker of the Sussex country lanes, usually covering around eight miles in a day. He preferred to wear old clothes, growing into them until he appeared more like a tramp than a well-to-do artist. He also became a health food fanatic, long before natural foods were fashionable, but he loved Amberley, and was jealous of its beauties.

Many artists and crafts people, particularly potters, have continued to choose Amberley for their homes and workshops over the years; providing tourists with souvenirs of the village long before such things were the norm.

Although Amberley is wonderful in the summer months, it can bring difficulties in winter with floods. Because of this Amberley folk were credited with being born with webbed feet. The women were once referred to as Yellow Bellies by those from neighbouring villages, supposedly because of their habit of lifting their skirts to warm themselves over smoky fires.

The Arun close by has always made Amberley popular with those who enjoy fishing and boating. One of Fuller's Seven Good Things of Sussex was an Amberley trout. During the 19th century, Angling competitions were very popular and as many as 800 anglers in special trains would descend upon sleepy little Amberley on Sundays.

There was a time when the village had several tradesmen and shopkeepers supplying almost all needs. In our car-dominated society, almost all of these have disappeared. A particular local industry was flint-picking, which was carried out by men on the farms in the areas. When the piles of flints were ready at the side of the fields, the pickers would load up their skid-boxes or skid-pans (made by the local blacksmiths), rather like sleighs, and haul them down to the roadside to be used for building, or for the roads.

Many other early skills may now be seen at the world famous Chalk Pits Museum which is on the site of the old lime burning quarries close to Amberley Railway Station.

One of Amberley's beautiful houses

Looking towards Amberley and its castle

PRETTY AND LEAFY BURY BY THE ARUN

To many Bury means just a Hill by that name on a road map, but to those who live there or know it well, it is as Nikolaus Pevsner describes it in his Buildings of England, a pretty and leafy place, although as another commentator noted it may be "rather too remote" for some.

The river Arun has always been important to Bury, although perhaps rather less so today than in the times when the waterway was a West Sussex artery of commerce. There are many memories of the Ferry from Bury to the Amberley side. Once the ferry was in the charge of a woman, a true Sussex character, Mrs. Shepherd, who had taken over from her husband rather than let it pass out of the family. She was replaced by her daughter, Mrs. Marshall who continued the family tradition.

The village has had some interesting residents. Galsworthy lived, and subsequently died at Bury House. He loved the place, and is said to have claimed a find of some gold dust hereabouts. There was also a local witch who turned herself into a hare at will, as these ladies often did. Or at least so the locals believed, especially the young girls who consulted her to enquire about their future husbands.

In more recent times there was Mabel Constanduros, remembered for her chronicles of the infamous Buggins family. She lived at Prattenden's Cottage, which she had fallen in love with at first glance.

The church which is 12th and 13th century, with later additions, is said to be on the sight of an earlier Saxon building. Of the church bells, there is one dedicated to St. Dunstan, which is said to be a Maiden Bell or one which when it was cast was so true in tone, that it did not require tuning. Legend has it that this bell was a gift from the Bury villagers, as an offering for their deliverance from a great storm. The bell is inscribed Sancte Bunstane Ora pro Nobis (St. Dunstan pray for us), and dates from about 1400.

Hilaire Belloc had a high regard for little Bury, and includes it in his Sussex Drinking Song. No great deeds to be recalled, but much charming local history, such as the wooden pattens worn by the Bury womenfolk because of the Sussex mud. They are remembered for the sound they made — clickety-clack, clickety-clack. Then there were the little carts drawn by dogs, which brought oil and fish from Littlehampton to the village until this was forbidden by law.

Any account of Bury would be incomplete without its own riddle — "Where was beer sold by the pound?" and a native would reply with glee, "At Bury surelee, because Nancy Green had a liddle shop whur she sold beer and other odds and ends, and it wur right beside the village pound".

A final word from Mabel Constanduros writing in 1947 "This part of the world is still unspoiled and lovely. Many of its houses have stood for two hundred years or more. The river winds peacefully on its way to the sea, and the yellow iris still blooms in spring on its banks. The little church and the Manor sleep side by side in the sunshine". Happily not too much has changed.

Bury — where they sold beer by the pound

View from Bury

The tiny hamlet of Stopham, four miles from Petworth, has just a church and a few houses in a cul-de-sac. But this is wonderful Wealden countryside, and as if to make up for the lack of any other attractions there is the dream-like medieval bridge across the river, which has often been called the best bridge of its period in Sussex.

The bridge is on the site of the ancient Eastover Ferry which belonged to John Stopham. It replaced the ferry in 1309 and was rebuilt in stone in the early fifteenth century. The raised centre arch, to permit the passage of barges, dates from 1822, but the other arches are all original. It is of course a listed building, so presumably it will now remain intact for posterity.

St. Mary's Church at Stopham is an interesting early Norman building, with the monuments and tombs of the Barttelot family, who were the owners of the big house nearby. It was said that the Barttelots could ride from Stopham to Horsham without once leaving their own land.

Rectors of the church were noted for their longevity, but it was Thomas Newcombe, a poet as well as the Rector who beat all others. He remained in this lovely spot for sixty years, a tribute to the people and the parish.

In the days when oxen were seen as a normal part of Sussex agriculture, a Sussex newspaper of 1796 reported a ploughing match near Stopham Bridge between oxen and horses. It is not recorded who the victors were, although horses continued on Sussex farms longer than the humble bullock.

Ebernoe has always been a remote spot, and not only geographically. It was said that this little place defied the introduction of British Summer Time longer than anywhere else in the country. There is no pub, no shops, and not much else apart from the church of the Holy Trinity, built in 1967 which Nairn and Pevsner describe rather unkindly as a "tiny box-of-bricks chapel".

The village really comes alive once a year on July 25th (St. James' Day) when as many as two-to-three thousand people have been known to descend upon the Common for the annual Ebernoe Horn Fair.

The main event of the Fair is a cricket match between Ebernoe and a neighbouring village. This culminates in the presentation of the horns of a sheep, which has been roasted at the Fair, to the top scorer. The exact significance of the presentation, and indeed the origins of the Fair itself, have been lost in time. It would certainly appear that the event is very old, although it was revived in 1864 after it had lapsed for some time.

The history of any ancient custom is normally punctuated with periods of decline followed by revivals, and Horn Fairs with long histories are known in several places. Folklorists have written at great length on the use of horns as a trophy. A saying is "Alls fair at Horn Fair", although this may apply to another fair rather than Ebernoe.

A storm on Fair Day is essential to bring good luck and good crops in the ensuing year, and gardeners are exhorted to sow their cabbages on Fair Day.

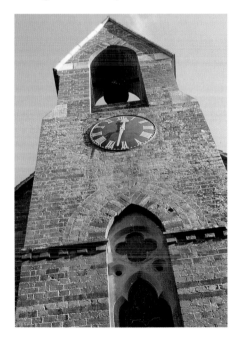

Ebernoe church and its clock

The beautiful old bridge at Stopham near Pulborough

Billingshurst, about six miles from Horsham, is a main road village which is fast becoming a small town — or perhaps this has already happened. Fortunately it still retains much of its village character, in spite of modern trappings such as a car park and shopping precinct.

The Parish Church of St. Mary stands above the main road, where since its origins in the 13th century, it has observed the comings and goings of the locals about their daily work, whether it be sheep droving or fast driving. The church once had six bells, and this must have had something to do with the name of the local hostelry Ye Olde Six Bells. Since 1892 the church has had eight bells, but the pub has kept its original name.

There is also an old Unitarian Chapel, dating from 1754, with an unexpectedly large churchyard. This is one of the oldest chapels of this kind in Southern England, and during its life it has seen much history and several changes. In 1880 the Baptistery was turned into a Library and Schoolroom and the long table used then still survives.

On Shrove Tuesday each year, in celebration of the last day before Lent, the old sport (so-called) of cock-throwing was once observed in the village. As the name implies this was a cruel practice, with nothing whatever in its favour. When it finally came to an end, it was the Pastor of the Unitarian Chapel who had a lot to do with its passing, when he penned a powerful poem against the game.

Another old custom which is still kept up annually in Billingshurst, is the November 5th bonfire. It was once the practice of a man taking the part of the devil, to run up the side of the bonfire whilst the villagers recited their Bonfire Hymn. The pretend devil was badly burned one year, so this particular part of the proceedings was stopped.

Newbridge, between the two villages of Billingshurst and Wisborough Green, will be familiar to anyone who has studied the history of the Wey and Arun Canal and its junction with the Arun river. The area is well known for flooding during winter months.

Wisborough Green has as its name implies, a fine village green, nicely encircled by trees. There are some satisfying cottages in Wealden style, and the obligatory village pond. A local belief is that none can claim to be a true resident of Wisborough Green until they have fallen (or have been pushed) into the pond at least once.

The church of St. Peter ad Vincula, includes parts from several centuries starting with the 11th, but was rather poorly restored in 1867. A huge stone altar was removed and hidden during less happy times, but was thankfully returned to the church in 1937. This was once a well known place of pilgrimage, and held several relics of the saints including, it was claimed, the cloak of St. Thomas a Becket.

Autumn day on the green at Wisborough Green

Floods at Newbridge between Billingshurst and Wisborough Green

VILLAGE WAS JEFFERIES' CHOICE

Goring, was once a self-contained village to the west of Worthing, but is now very much a part of the enlarged town, having lost its village status in the house-building boom after the First World War. It has always been noted for its profusion of trees, although many of these were sacrificed to the builders. The beach was once virgin foreshore, but is now part of the tripper's sea front which begins at Worthing and continues to Littlehampton. As Gerard Young said in The Cottage in the Fields (1945) "Rural tracks and lanes down to the beach have lost their tranquillity and have become elongated car parks, and where the seagulls used to cry in their lonely search over the sands, they now compete with the tricycle bell of the ice-cream man".

The cheerful Parish Church of St. Mary was largely rebuilt by Decimus Burton in 1837 although older parts of the nave remain. It has been unkindly said that the church is best seen from a distance.

Boats and bathing huts at Goring

The nature writer Richard Jefferies chose to spend the last years of his life at Goring, living at Sea View, since re-named Jefferies House. He died in 1887 being buried as was that other great country writer W.H. Hudson, in Broadwater churchyard. Was it the amount of green trees along the Goring lanes that persuaded Jefferies to settle in this pleasant place? Before the turn of the century Goring must have had more of the character of a village. A writer in the Sussex County Magazine in 1927 recalled Squire Stanhope driving around the Goring lanes with his silver hair black ribboned into a pig tail. At harvest the men sang:

Our wives and sweethearts we regale,
With home spun jest and nut brown ale,
Laddie-tum-day, Laddie-tum-day
We'll all go make the new mown hay.

At around this period the lane from Goring to Worthing had a barn on the north side, which was said to be haunted. Horses passing this spot would swerve to the opposite side of the road, and sometimes it meant turning back and making for home by a circuitous route. Of course the old barn has long gone, and the lane now a wide road, is apparently freed from any evil influences.

Like many sea coast villages, Goring had it tales of smugglers. At Sea Place a soldier was shot dead by a member of the infamous Hawkhurst Gang in an ambush in the 18th century, when the smugglers were bringing contraband ashore. Such deeds are still recalled by the name Smugglers Walk although the Hawkhurst Gang were broken up in 1749.

Many visitors now come to Goring to visit the R.C. Church of the English Martyrs. Not so much to see the church itself which is unremarkable, but to gaze in wonder at local artist Gary Bevan's reproduction of the Sistine Chapel Ceiling which completely covers the inside roof of the church. The artist began his labour of love in 1988 after a visit to Rome. It is now completed although additions to the walls still have to be added. The medium used was an acrylic-based paint, but the colours are completely authentic to match the restored ceiling of the original.

Early morning and a deserted beach

Canon Palmer wrote in 1862 "I know of no more beautiful view than that one from our Downs just at this time of year; on a day like this: a delicate blue haze in the distance, just not obscuring the sea..." . The Rev. George and the late Rev. Henry Palmer, father and son, between them filled the rectorship of Sullington for over a century, and the beautiful views from this lovely Sussex spot may have had a lot to do with their reluctance to leave it. From the heights of Sullington Warren, which has been compared to Scotland, it is possible to see Leith Hill to the North, the Hampshire Downs to the West and Devil's Dyke to the East.

Sullington is not even a village, really just a church, a farmyard and beautiful scenery. The cul-de-sac from the main road ends with the farmyard, which is dominated by a huge tithe barn, 115 feet long. This is very special and can be counted as one of the most important buildings in Sussex. There is a timber which proudly states 1685, although it is believed that this only dates from when the barn was restored at one point in its long history. It is still a working barn, and is also sometimes used for real Sussex Barn Dances, for which it provides tremendous authentic atmosphere. One other interesting bit of history is that the barn once housed machinery which provided electricity for the buildings close by, before the electricity generating companies were formed.

The church of St. Mary is almost like a farm building, basically Saxon but with later details. From the approach road it appears to be part of the farmyard, as the buildings nestle up to each other so neatly. There is a life size monument of a Knight in chain mail of the time of Henry III — rather mutilated now but it can still claim to be the oldest stone monument in Sussex. The Knight is thought to be a De Covert, possibly Sir William, who was Lord of the Manor in the 13th century.

Like so many other lovely Sussex places, Sullington inspired poets such as Arthur Bell:

Up above Sullington, watching my sheep,
I felt the noon grow still,
The bee on the thyme-flower droned asleep,
And the cloud-shadow stayed on the hill.

Pulborough has not yet really decided whether to be a large village or a small town. With the luxury of a railway station on a line untouched by Beeching, its many London commuters will probably soon make sure that it becomes the latter. The church is charmingly simple, with contributions from many centuries. It is adorned by a lovely lychgate with a Horsham stone roof, one of many such gates in West Sussex.

The river has always been a very important part of Pulborough, particularly where anglers are concerned. The Pulborough eels which were included in the Seven Good Things of Sussex, were said to grow to a tremendous size.

Treasure is supposed to be buried under the Mound, which probably was once topped with a Roman fort, and fairy funerals were supposed to be seen here, in the days when Sussex folk firmly believed in The Pharisees. More tangible history has been provided by the large quantity of Roman artefacts which have been uncovered in this area over the years.

Sullington Church – close to the old farmyard

Water Meadows at Pulborough

FISHING VILLAGE TO SOUTH COAST RESORT

Before the eighteenth century Worthing was an obscure fishing village, most often described as 'a hamlet of Broadwater'. The buildings would have consisted of a few miserable huts, plus a handful of houses which did not exceed forty shillings a year in rental. The adjoining ground could have been purchased for the value of five gallons of brandy.

But things were to change during the last quarter of the 18th century, when it became a fashionable seaside holiday resort following in the wake of neighbouring Brighton. Not that it could ever aspire to quite the same degree of popularity, but for those who desired a little more quiet and seclusion, then Worthing definitely had its attractions.

The trend was firmly set in 1797 when Her Royal Highness Princess Amelia decided on Worthing as her favourite Summer residence. By 1803 the streets of Worthing were being widened and well lit, and it was dignified with name of Town. All this was followed in 1809 by the erection of a Market Hall and Chapel.

The gentle maritime climate has always been in Worthing's favour. Sheltered by the Downs, the town which lay on a level with the beach was usually much warmer and less inclined to extremes of weather than inland places less than 20 miles away. Residents who phone their friends a few miles away on the other side of the range of hills are often surprised by the difference in weather conditions. The town has for many years been a great favourite with older folk who appreciate its mild climate and level roads. The weather is normally so mild that myrtle and fig trees grow to perfection and it was these conditions which brought about the pre-war proliferation of market gardens in the area.

Worthing Pier is the third such erection. The first was opened on 12th April 1862, as a simple deck with a landing stage at the pierhead. It had been designed by Sir Robert Rawlinson a well known engineer. It had two small buildings at the shore end, one used as a bazaar and the other as the pier toll house. In 1881 shelters were added at the sea end, followed by a pavilion in 1888, which accommodated a bandstand and around 600 spectators. A string band played there for 3 hours daily, weather permitting, receiving the princely sum of five pounds between them as a salary.

In 1913 disaster struck the pier, when a very severe storm along the south coast reduced it to a twisted wreck, as many contemporary picture postcards show. The south pavilion was completely cut off, and was nicknamed Easter Island, with steamer trips being organised to take visitors out to it. The pier reopened in May 1914, but disaster struck again in 1933 when fire broke out in the south pavilion, completely destroying it. It was rebuilt again two years later in more modern style.

In 1940 the poor old pier had a hole blown in it to hinder any possible landing by German forces. It was finally joined up again in 1949. The remark has been made that the pier has been blown down, burnt out, and blown up, but in spite of it all has survived.

Worthing's Pier Pavilion

Worthing beach and pier in the evening light

OLD MOTHER GORING'S MANY MYSTERIES

Chanctonbury ring has been called the Monarch of Sussex Hills. It rises 700 feet above sea level, and as Hilaire Belloc said "sitting crowned in the middle place". The summit of the hill encompasses an Iron-age Hill Fort and within this the remains of a Roman Temple dating from around the 3rd or 4th centuries AD. Until the great storm of 1987, the Ring was embellished by a group of fine trees planted in 1760 by Charles Goring, whose family owned the site. At the time he was a young man, and it is recorded that he toiled up the hill day by day to water and tend the saplings. He hardly expected to be alive to see his labours rewarded by a group of mature trees, but in 1828 when he was in his eighties, he was able to write a poem which told us of his joy when he beheld the crown of the hill:

Oh! Could I live to see thy top, all in its beauty dress'd,

That time's arrived; I've had my wish, and lived to eighty-five,

I'll thank my God who gave such grace, as long as e'er I live.

Not that everyone was completely delighted with Charles' success. There were some who felt the Ring was better unadorned, and others who felt that such an open spot was not a suitable place for planting trees. Perhaps the latter were to some extent vindicated in 1987, although by that time most observers had grown to love the crown of this famous Sussex hill.

Wilfred Blunt was also moved to poetry when he looked at Chanctonbury:

Say what you will — there is not in the world,

a nobler sight than from this upper down,

No rugged landscape here, no beauty hurled

from its Creator's hand as with a frown,

but a green plain on which green hills look down.

Local folk also looked at the hill when they needed to know what the weather had in store. The saying was "Old Mother Goring's got her cap on, we shall have some wet". The lady's cap was the circle of mist which sometimes enveloped the upper part of the hill. But this was not the only bit of folklore connected with Chanctonbury Ring — in fact this spot might claim to be the most magical in the whole of Sussex, with a veritable anthology of folk beliefs connected with it . The Devil, fairies, ghosts and buried treasure. They are all here; with the best known story telling of how if you run around the summit seven times (a magical number) then his Satanic Majesty will emerge from the trees and offer you a bowl of soup (or milk) in return for your soul.

A Dew Pond has long been associated with Chanctonbury, although not always the same one. Opinions vary as to the age of these ponds — some say the first one here dated only from the 19th century, whilst other historians firmly believe in very much earlier origins.

Perhaps the greatest emotion evoked by the hill is the elation experienced on a clear day when it is possible to view five counties —Sussex, Surrey, Kent, Hampshire and Isle of Wight. And all around the green villages of the Sussex Weald.

View from the ring looking East

Chanctonbury's famous dew pond

Most people will agree that little Sussex churches like St. Botolphs are jewels to be treasured and guarded. It is difficult to realise that a relatively few years ago, this was not always so. The Sussex historian Thomas Horsfield writing in the 19th century dismissed this church as "small and uninteresting". Times and viewpoints change, and in 1970 another author felt compelled to devote around six pages to St. Botolph's church in a book on Saxon buildings.

The hamlet consists of the church and a few cottages and houses in the Adur Gap, south of Steyning. The population must have always been small, although at one time it was a thriving little community, rich in Sussex history. The 19th and 20th centuries have been rather unkind to this lovely spot, inflicting the railway line, a cement works, and electricity pylons all close by. But in some ways this has increased rather than spoilt the tranquillity.

The church is mainly Saxon, with a scratch dial near the porch, and some wall paintings which are said to be some of the oldest church paintings of this kind in the country. Once Sussex must have been particularly rich in churches with biblical pictures on their walls, and before many folk could read these were known as the Bible of the people, until in 1547 an Act of Parliament decreed that they should all be obliterated. Thankfully many survived, at least to some extent, and may be viewed today. The St. Botolph paintings are thought to be of many periods, in layers one on another, but with the earliest dating from Saxon times.

Once the church is said to have contained statues of the Blessed Virgin, St. Peter and St. Botolph. We believe that the original dedication of the church was to St. Mary, but in 1520 John Slutter left instructions that he should be buried "in the church of Bottolys, giving to St. Peter's Lyght, to the Lyght of Our Ladye and the Lyght of St. Botollys a yew sheep".

Although not mentioned in the Domesday under its present name, Annington (spelt Hangingedune) is there, and this was almost certainly the same area.

Roman bricks found near the village have been thought by some historians to be part of an ancient bridge mentioned in old papers. Even in the twelfth century the bridge was referred to as old, so it may have been a Roman structure. But this is now a mystery of which we can only guess at the solution.

The Lyghts which once burnt before the saints' statues may be missing from the church today, but the light of Christianity in Sussex still burns brightly even in tiny churches like St. Botolphs. Arthur Stanley in his Off the Beaten Track in Sussex described it thus: "St. Botolph's is a half-way house of God, within whose walls one is well content to rest awhile".

St. Botolph's Church

The interior of the old Saxon church of St. Botolphs

The village of Sompting lies two miles to the north of Worthing, although modern buildings have almost joined the two together. The smaller place, mentioned in Domesday as Sulinges, still has a few of its original flint and brick dwellings struggling for survival amongst the 20th century bungalows. But it also has a rare treasure in the little church of St Mary on the edge of the village, and at the very start of the Downs. What makes this church unique is its wonderful Saxon tower, the only one of its kind in the country. The cap of the tower is known to the experts as a Rhenish Helm, to tie in with similar church towers found in German Rhineland. The complete church although quite early, is also very elegant. The tower can be dated back to at least the 11th century, and the rest of the church has a history of nearly 900 years.

The carvings on the tower and stone fragments in the church are important as true examples of such an early period in church construction. The building was granted to the Knights Templars in 1154, when reconstruction took place. At this time a little chapel was built specifically for the use of the Knights. Squabbles within the church are nothing new, and in 1306 the Knights Templars were out of favour, and the church was passed to the Knights of St. John, who also built themselves a chapel.

This area is an important one to archaeologists, many Roman remains having been discovered, including early jewellery. In the realm of folklore Sompting is said to have its treacle mines, just as Faygate has in the north of the county. The Chanctonbury Morris Men give their performance of the local Mummers Play in the car park of a Sompting pub, each Boxing Day morning, later repeating it at Steyning.

Although so small, Sompting has always had a number of important visitors and residents. One of the most distinguished of the latter was Edward John Trelawney, an adventurer of the old school, with as the name implies, a Cornish background. He was on the shore when the boat carrying Shelley perished, and it was Trelawney, Byron and Leigh Hunt who cremated the poet's body ten days later. He snatched Shelley's heart from the fire and gave it to the poet's wife, also providing the widow with sufficient funds to return to England. The following year Trelawney went to Greece with Byron to help the Greeks in their war of independence from Turkey. The last five years he spent in rural Britain, firstly in South Wales and latterly in Sompting. He died here in his 89th year.

Sompting church lies close to the old Downland road to Steyning, which provides a dramatic ride even by modern transport. The great Sussex author Hilaire Belloc wrote of "The great hills of the South Country, they stand along the sea. And it's there walking in the high woods, that I could wish to be ". Belloc was an individualist, and did not always express in his writings the feelings of the majority. But in his attitude to his beloved Sussex Downs, he echoed in praise and verse, the feelings of many who live close by, as well as others who had strayed far away. For Sussex folk in foreign parts (and anywhere outside of Sussex is "furrin" to the true Sussex dweller), the Downs written about so eloquently by Belloc, Kipling, and many others, are the true heart of Sussex — even more so than the Coast or the Weald. A quote from Harrison Ainsworth says it all : "No hills can be more beautiful than these Sussex Downs. They may want height, boldness, grandeur, sublimity; they possess not forest, rock torrent or ravine; but they have gentleness, softness and other endearing attributes. Regarded in combination with each other, the high ranges form an exquisite picture".

The unmistakeable outline of Sompting Church steeple

Downland patterns near Steyning

Bramber, although consisting almost entirely of one short street, is not without character and charm — in spite of one famous writer who complained of "nothing to see". In 1813 it was described as a '"mean village with 22 houses, 91 inhabitants and 2 Members of Parliament". At that period it was one of the notorious Rotten boroughs and a much-told tale concerns William Wilberforce who only passed through the place but once and is supposed to have remarked "Why that must be the place I'm the Member for".

The remains of the Castle, although insignificant as Sussex castles go, have a certain dignity. The fragment of the Tower Keep, 76 feet high, is in the care of the National Trust, who wisely do little except keep it tidy. Thus it remains an honest and sturdy remnant of the past, without any pretensions of romance for the tourist market.

The Castle was listed in Domesday, so this confirms its Saxon origin. It was long the residence of the de Braose family, who must have relished the views of a wide sweep of the Downs. Who originally built it or why, we know not, and exactly when it fell we know almost as little. An engraving of the site, dating from the 17th century shows almost the same view as today. It has been suggested that its disintegration owed something to the use of gunpowder, but the elements coupled with the local's depredations for their own building needs, cannot be discounted.

There are many legends attached to the Castle. The most dramatic is the story of four young children who were imprisoned and starved to death, and whose wraiths have appeared ever since begging for food. Another equally disturbing story is of Maud of Ditchling and her lover William de Lindfield. The latter was starved in a dungeon by Hubert de Hurst, Maud's husband, who found William embracing his wife. Maud died of a broken heart, and her husband a raving lunatic.

The church of St. Nicholas was built, not as a Parish Church, but as a chapel for the castle about 1075, when the Benedictines established a small college there. The church continued to serve the castle and the village and the seafarers who sailed up the arm of the sea to Bramber Quay. This was in the days when the water came right up to the edge of the Castle hill. The Bridge which spanned the water at Bramber was said to have been about 170ft. wide. Bramber was at that time an important Sussex port and had been so since before Domesday.

All that now remains of the old castle at Bramber

God's acre at Bramber

The picturesque town of Steyning lies in the valley formed by the river Adur as it make its way to the sea at Shoreham. Our Saxon ancestors called it Steningham (from Stean — meaning Stone) and in the Domesday Survey it is given as Staninges. So obviously Steyning is an old town with plenty of interesting history; in fact once it was far more important than today, with a harbour and its own Mint.

It is close by the Downs, so sheep played a large part in its commerce, as implied by Sheep Pen Lane. Cattle were also important with a fortnightly market held in the main street on Mondays. There were also sheep and cattle sold at the three annual fairs in June, September and October.

Steyning has an absolute wealth of vernacular architecture, and will repay more than one visit by anyone interested in this subject. Many of the most attractive buildings are in the High Street which runs North-West, and in Church Street, which branches off from it and has the Grammar School founded in 1614.

Also in Church Street is the charming little timber-framed Saxon Cottage. It is not actually as early as the name suggest, but is probably 16th century. It is made entirely without nails, and has a thatched roof and a steep cat-slide almost to the ground, a contrast to the many other houses roofed with Horsham stone slabs. It is now owned by the National Trust and was for a time used by the Steyning Museum to house some of it exhibits. One of the firms who make miniatures of English country cottages produced a very fine facsimile of Saxon Cottage some years ago, although they gave it a different name.

The church of St. Andrew is believed to stand on the site of a much earlier church, built by St. Cuthman. The present church was almost certainly once much bigger, but it is still magnificent within and well worth a return visit if locked at the first attempt. There are two Sanctuary Rings on the church door which in the past gave protection to fugitives. King Ethulwulf, father of Alfred the Great, was said to be buried here, as was Steyning's own private saint, Cuthman. There is even an old gravestone pointed out as his actual grave. St. Cuthman's day is February 8th, and some of the legends woven around his life appear in a charming play by Christopher Fry The Boy with the Cart.

In the High Street is the Old Market House with its little clock turret. This building has been put to numerous uses. Elections have been held in it, the Quakers used it for meetings, it functioned as the Town Hall in 1835, and from 1896 to 1936 it was the fire station. The clock once held sway above the pigeon loft at Michelgrove near Arundel, but when this mansion was demolished in 1860 the clock passed to Steyning.

A little masterpiece, Steyning's clock tower

Sussex country architecture at its best in Steyning

West Grinstead, halfway between Horsham and the Downs, is not really a village in the formal sense, although it has two churches, both of more than passing interest. The church of St. George is a long way from any habitation, but close to the river Adur. It has been suggested that in past times worshippers came by barge or boat to attend services. During the last century the river at this point was used as a canal, with locks and a turning point about half a mile west of the church. A local tradition says that crusading Knights Templars passed down the river from Shipley on their way to the sea at Shoreham.

St. George's church is not mentioned in Domesday, although the earliest part must have been built soon afterwards. The church like so many others has been rebuilt and added to through the centuries, with the squat tower dominating it since the 13th century. Of interest are the names of local farms lettered on the back of the pews — these were reserved for the men; women and children having to make do at the back of the church.

There are also many memorials, including one to William Powlett and his wife (1746) who is said by some to be the Squire Powlett who minus his head, haunts St. Leonards Forest; although the reason for this has never been explained.

Sir William Burrell lived at West Grinstead Park in the 18th century, and is best remembered for his important collection of Sussex documents and drawings which he left to the British Museum. The Burrell family included ironmasters, MPs and Squires through the years. In the churchyard are the graves of two family servants; one who joined the family when he was eight and another when he was 17, both stayed with the Burrells faithfully for 61 years.

In West Grinstead Park is the oak tree under which Pope is said to have written much of The Rape of the Lock. Another tree, this one a maple, was supposed to have the gift of bestowing long life on any child passed through its branches.

Not far away is the lovely little Roman Catholic church of Our Lady of Consolation and St. Francis. This was the church attended by Hilaire Belloc when he lived at Shipley. Some of the local people still remember him in his distinctive black cloak attending Mass, often accompanied by his friend G.K. Chesterton. He wrote "Sussex, may your earth cover me, and may some priest from Arundel or Grinstead have sung above my bones". In fact he got his wish and was buried here; his memorial may be seen next to the tower door of the church.

Beside the Catholic church is the 18th century Priest House. This is of particular interest because it incorporates a much earlier cottage which had a secret chapel, used by the Carylls, a local Catholic family, during less ecumenical times. In 1925 two chalices were found under the floor, one from the 15th century and one from the 17th. It is assumed that these were used by travelling priests who celebrated Mass for the Carylls in their hidden chapel.

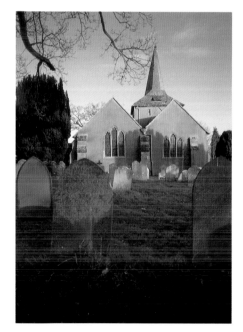

West Grinstead church and its squat stone tower

The heart of the Sussex Weald

Horsham has had a long and chequered history, in spite of surprisingly not meriting a mention in the Domesday survey. Until relatively modern times it was an assize town and also an important market centre, serving the country villages for many miles around. It had a population of 3,000 at the start of the nineteenth century and this has steadily grown until it is now home to ten times as many.

The town gaol was on Goal Green (once part of the Carfax) and later in Queen Street on the east side of the town. Public executions took place on Horsham Common, a large open area to the North. These were considered a great family day-out and were attended by all kinds of cheap-jacks and

One of Horsham's oldest houses, its bright white exterior belying its age

ballad sellers, until more humanitarian views prevailed in the middle of the last century. The last man to be publicly hanged in Horsham was in the year 1844. Smuggling was a popular industry, with runs of contraband goods being brought up from the coast to Horsham, where they were distributed and sold. Unlike other crimes, smuggling was not considered particularly anti-social and the smuggling gangs operated with the tacit approval of many otherwise law-abiding and god-fearing townsfolk.

Fairs were held regularly in the town from 1233 when a charter was granted by Henry III. During most of the 19th century, fairs, circuses and bonfires took place on the Carfax, the large open space in the middle of Horsham. In 1874 the very popular July Fair was reduced to one day, and in 1886 it was abolished completely — although later fairs in the Jews Meadows on the west side of the town were still held each year in July. The removal of such events from the Carfax must have been greatly welcomed by the townsfolk who lived around the perimeter, and who had suffered much whenever the itinerants set up shop close to their dwellings. The Carfax then became much more organised and respectable, with a bandstand being erected in 1892.

Still a very lovely part of the town, the tree-lined Causeway leads to the Parish Church of St. Mary the Virgin and past this to the infant river Arun, and the cricket field. The church is a mixture of 13th, 14th and 15th century work and has often been described as one of the finest in West Sussex. It was restored in 1864-5 at a cost of £8,000.

Horsham has changed tremendously, particularly in the last few years, but the Causeway has remained virtually unscathed. The collection of houses of different periods are all a joy, many of them roofed with the distinctive Horsham stone slabs. These can also be seen underfoot beside the roadway. Once this road was noted for its bad surface, and pedestrians were given stepping stones of Horsham slabs to cross from one side to the other.

Part of the splendid façade of Horsham's Causeway

MILL AND MEETING HOUSE — BODY AND SOUL

Sussex has been fortunate in its literary giants, and most will agree that one of the greatest was Hilaire Belloc, who was born in France in 1870 to a French father and English mother. He spent much of his childhood however in Slindon, and here he discovered that Sussex was his true spiritual home. It was in 1906, the year in which he became a Liberal Member of Parliament, that he purchased Shipley Mill and the house Kings Land which nestled beneath it. At the time Shipley village consisted of a collection of scattered cottages and farms, in what was some of the finest open country of the Weald. Belloc evidently fell in love with Mrs Shipley, as some of the locals called the mill, and several tales are told of his delight when he first moved into the house.

The first Christmas at Shipley, the Bellocs arranged a children's party in the mill itself, and erected a magnificent Christmas tree on the first floor. As the children hopped and danced around the tree in delight, Belloc is said to have stood transfixed with wide-eyed wonder at the scene. This was typical of this enigmatic man, who could be so dogmatic and unyeilding in many things and yet could take on the mantle of childhood when involved with something connected with his beloved Sussex.

Although an adopted man of Sussex, Belloc had his fair share of Sussex obstinacy. He also respected this in others and told with evident satisfaction how often he tried to persuade his old Sussex gardener to do things scientifically and how the old chap promptly reverted to his own ways as soon as his master's back was turned. Another example of this Sussex trait, may be seen at Dragons Green, close to Shipley, where at the George and Dragon pub there is a tombstone in the front garden. This dates from 1893 when the albino son of the pub's landlord died after a lifetime of ridicule at the hands of a group of locals. During the funeral at the church and later on the gravestone his mother and father gave vent to their feelings about his wretched life. The vicar objected, and rather than give in, the parents had their son's stone moved from the churchyard to the garden of the pub where it remains to this day — a splendid example of the Sussex refusal to "be druv".

Not far away from Shipley, between Bilingshurst and Coolham, is the strangely named Blue Idol. Just as Belloc's mill once provided food for the body, then this lovely building may be said to have provided refreshment for the soul. It was originally part of a Tudor farmhouse, converted in 1691 by the great Quaker William Penn, for use as a Meeting House for the local Friends. Honest and plain, like all things Quaker, it is still in use today as a haven of peace and spiritual renewal.

Many different suggestions have been offered for the origin of the name, which appears to date only from the 19th century — before this it was known simply as the Old House. It seems unlikely that we will ever really know how it came by its present name, but no one would want to change it.

The strangely named Blue Idol at Coolham

The beautiful Smock Mill at Shipley

In 1823 Cobbett called it "A most villainous track" and very much earlier the Venerable Bede had talked about the Sussex forests as being "Thick and inaccessible". This is the most westerly of the four forests which once stretched across the central Weald of Sussex; part of the great forest area known to the Romans as Anderida and to the Saxons as Andredeswald. It is bounded by Horsham, Crawley and the villages of Lower Beeding and Handcross, with Faygate, Colgate, Pease Pottage, and Mannings Heath as actual forest villages.

In Roman times iron was worked here, and in rather more modern times the casting of the first iron cannon in 1543, stimulated the wealden iron industry. As one old rhyme had it:

Master Huggett and his man John,

They did cast the first cannon.

By the late 17th century, the forests were no longer the Black Country of Sussex, and nature once more took over. The most enduring, and indeed the most picturesque remains of the iron industry, are the furnace ponds. They bear such names as Hawkins Pond — said to be named after a smuggler, Roosthole Pond and of course Hammer Pond.

In 1794 Arthur Young described the forest of St. Leonard as "Waste land producing nothing but rabbits". Cobbett in 1823 obviously agreed with him. But not everyone felt the same way. There were those who delighted in the inaccessibility and its vast array of flora and fauna. The wolves and wild boar of earlier times had disappeared, but there were still the herds of deer roaming free, as they still do today. The sandstone found in the forest was also appreciated for its properties as a building material, being used in the construction of Horsham Town Hall, and the wall around Horsham Park.

We have no idea how the forest got its name, as there is no firm evidence that a Saint named Leonard ever visited it. Not the least of the many attractions of the forest are the folk tales and legends which emanate from it. The best known is about this mysterious saint who is said to have fought and killed a fearsome dragon here. The tale is proven by the fact that wherever the saint's blood was spilt in the fight, a lily of the valley bloomed and many such plants can still be found today. It is now designated as an Area of Outstanding Natural Beauty and there are several nature reserves.

A more recent dragon story is told in a broadsheet of 1614 which speaks of a beast nine feet or more in length and shaped in the form of an axletree of a cart. It was seen within half a mile of Horsham and was most terrible and noisome to the inhabitants. The broadsheet fails to tell us whether the dragon was eventually despatched.

A mile long avenue within the forest is known as Mick Miles (or Mike Mills) Race. Here Mick, who was a smuggler ran a race with the Devil; the prize being the smuggler's soul. Needless to say Mick won, but only by a whisker. Tradition states that no vegetation will ever grow along The Race.

Another enduring legend is of Squire Paullett, a headless spectre who delighted in leaping on the back of your horse, always supposing you were unwise enough to venture into the forest after dark. Other legends are of Charles II hiding in a yew tree and being offered Pease-Pudding by an old lady who lived close by; and a more believable tale of a Black Princess, who was in fact Mrs. Helena Bennett a Persian aristocrat who retired to Colgate Lodge and is buried in Horsham Parish Churchyard.

St. Leonards Forest near Horsham

Roost Hole pond in St. Leonard' Forest

Henfield, a downland village (or perhaps town) halfway between Horsham and Brighton, has ancient origins. It was included in the Domesday survey under the almost familiar name of Hamfelde, meaning a settlement or village on open ground or field. It must have been relatively sleepy until the 18th century, when improved roads encouraged expansion. The river Adur to the north of the parish was busy with coal barges coming up to the Mock bridge, until the coming of the railway, which served Henfield well, until the branch line was closed in 1966.

There are many nice old buildings interspersed with newer ones. Particularly noteworthy are the cottages at the south-east end of the common, which is on either side of the main Brighton Road as it takes off from Henfield at Golden Square. Cricket is still played here, providing an archetypal Sussex village scene. The game of Quoits, which fell out of popularity in the 1920s was also played on the Green.

There is a local charity or Dole, Dame Gresham's Charity, which originated in Henfield on All-Hallows Day (November 1st) over 300 years ago, and which is still carried on. The good lady Gresham was a member of the local family of Byshopp, and she left in her will instructions that profits from a field of seven acres should be used to clothe some of the poor of Henfield. During World War II, clothing vouchers were substituted, but the charity is now once again observed in the traditional way in the church.

From the same family was Henry Byshopp, the first Postmaster General after the restoration of Charles II and the man generally considered to be the originator of our modern postal system.

The village once had many local trades and crafts. One of the more unusual was the large-scale cultivation of violets, which up to the 1920s were still being exported to many different countries.

The stories surrounding Henfield's famous Cat House have been told many times, but they are so unusual that it is worth recounting them once more. The house in question has a charming collection of black cats forever playing with canaries, painted onto the walls under the eaves. The origin of this unusual form of decoration goes back to the 19th century, when the cottage, originally called Leeches was the home of Bob Ward, a local eccentric.

Close by lived Canon Nathaniel Woodard, founder of the Woodard Schools. For some unknown reason these two gentlemen fell out and their dislike of each other came to a head when a cat belonging to the Canon killed a canary owned by Ward. The outrage so incensed the latter that he made effigies of cats and a string of scallop shells and hung these around his house, rattling them by means of a string whenever the cleric passed by. He is even supposed to have fired off a cannon in his garden.

Henfield's famous Cat House

An un-Sussex like view of Henfield

Little Cowfold is one of the many delightful villages of the Sussex Weald with no great buildings apart from the Parish Church and surprisingly a huge Carthusian Monastery. These apart, the village is full of pretty cottages, not least of which are the group facing inward towards the churchyard, with access from the road only at the rear. It would scarcely be an exaggeration to call this scene the most beautiful in Cowfold. The fence around the churchyard has the names of some of the local farms, noting who was responsible for the upkeep of that particular portion of God's Acre. The Village Hall of 1896 has received many well deserved accolades for its pleasing architecture.

The church is dedicated to St. Peter, and like many Sussex churches consists of parts from several different periods, but all charmingly simple. We know that there was a church here from at least 1232, when 'William' was the vicar. The simple font dates from 1481, and the tower from the same century. The church registers begin in 1588, and were once stored in a wonderful 16th century muniment chest. Victorian 'restoration' in 1876 swept away the gallery, the Georgian pews and the three decker pulpit.

One of the largest monumental brasses in Sussex is in the church, although sadly (but wisely) now kept out of sight. It is dedicated to a monk, Thomas Nelond. He was the XXVI Prior of St. Pancras, Lewes, and apparently a mighty man. The whole brass is nine feet ten inches long by four feet eight inches wide!

There was once a charity or dole in Cowfold, founded by Cecilia Heald in 1735, to provide bread for the poor of the Parish. The sum left for this purpose was a mere £26, but because this was not distributed until 1766, it accumulated with interest to £37-10s-0d — but that bought a lot of bread in the eighteenth century!

Visitors to this area may be surprised to notice a tall spire (200 feet high) through the trees on the southern border of Cowfold. It is not a cathedral strangely transplanted to the countryside, but the first sight of the beautiful group of buildings known as St. Hugh's Charterhouse, or more popularly Cowfold Monastery. Named by an unknown writer The Gate of Heaven it is the Sussex home of a community of Carthusian monks, who originated in Chartreuse nearly nine centuries ago.

The building started in 1876, with around 600 workmen of various nationalities being employed. Kilns on the site produced 60,000 bricks a fortnight. The foundation stone was laid in 1877, and the church consecrated in 1883. The little village, for such it really was, had been built to accommodate 80 monks, some of them priests and some lay brothers. Now sadly the numbers are much depleted, although the monastery still continues with its life of prayer and penance for those who embrace this form of Christian commitment.

Michael Fairless, the female author of that strange Sussex book The Roadmender, called the monks The Beadsmen of St. Hugh, and their distinctive white-robed figures may still be seen occasionally in the lanes around Cowfold.

The spire of St. Hugh's monastery rising to heaven

Cowfold Parish Church in its idyllic surroundings

SHOREHAM — OLD AND NEW

Shoreham is really two places, designated Old and New. In Domesday it appeared as Soresham, and it was not until the 13th century that the two distinct parts of the town are documented. In the 19th century a writer observed "Much cannot be said laudatory of the town — but it has its harbour, a source of wealth which neither Brighton or Worthing can boast of". And it is the harbour at New Shoreham which has brought fame and fortune to the town over the centuries. The river Adur has been important to this part of Sussex at least since the Norman Conquest, and by the 13th century Shoreham was being spoken as one of the most valuable harbours in the country. At this period Shoreham was expected to provide the Royal Navy with 26 vessels, a larger number than either Bristol, Newcastle or London.

Later its importance declined due to several causes, most connected with the continual problem of coastal drift. By the 18th century things had improved and a commentator wrote thus: "Shoreham; a sea-faring town and chiefly inhabited by ship-carpenters, ship-chandlers, and all the several trades depending upon the building and fitting up of ships, which is their chief business; and they are famed for neat building and for building good sea boats; that is to say, ships that are wholesome in the sea.

Perhaps because of the traditional nature of its main occupations Shoreham was, and still to some extent is, an old fashioned sort of place. Undoubtedly this is its great charm. Perhaps it is a little unfair to note that a traveller returning from the Australian colonies in 1901, considered the town almost the same as when he left it in 1840s only "a trifle more drowsy". However he did note one change — the disappearance of the sign over a shop in the High Street which read:

Here he lives, old Uncle Nat,
Try his oysters, fresh and fat,
Full-roed herrings ready to burst,
Table beer to quench your thirst.

The old lighthouse, which was built as long ago as 1846, still remains, a symbol of the enduring nature of Shoreham's sea-faring character. In 1918, two huge, mysterious towers were constructed near the lighthouse by the Royal Engineers. Because we were still at war, local folk were not told what they were to be used for, and many theories, wild and wonderful, circulated. They were in fact intended for the defence of the Straits of Dover but because of the end of hostilities, they were never used in this way. One was towed out to the Solent, and the other remained until 1924 when it was finally dismantled, after the Harbour trustees threatened to charge the government harbour dues.

Shoreham beach was originally a bungalow town, much favoured by theatricals and other assorted characters. Many of the bungalows were old converted railway carriages and because of open fires and oil lamps and the wooden construction there were several bad house fires. The bohemian lifestyle was abruptly halted by the war — in 1940 the residents were given orders to evacuate the Beach area within 48 hours. The army then proceeded to demolish many of the bungalows as an anti-invasion measure. Since the war much new building has taken place and now Shoreham Beach is a fashionable residential area, whilst the harbour once noted for its import of such commodities as timber and coal, is now equally popular with private pleasure craft.

Shoreham beach and lighthouse

Shoreham's forest of boats

Fulking is a tiny place two and a half miles from Bramber, where nothing seems to happen, although the very air is redolent of old Sussex and its motto "We wunt be druv".

The most photographed bit of Fulking is the roadside fountain erected by a local brewer to the memory of John Ruskin. When Arthur Beckett, editor of the old Sussex County Magazine visited it in the early part of this century, many of the ornamental tiles from the front of the fountain were missing. When he asked a Fulking native for the reason he was told "That was done by the frostes, sir. Very good water, sir. It comes from the 'ills, and don't see the light till it comes from that 'ere spout".

The text is displayed in Victorian tiles (one letter per tile) and reads:

He sendeth springs into the valley which run among the hills,

Oh that men would praise the Lord for his goodness

A curiosity is that some of the letter tiles have been inserted upside down, but luckily these are all of the letter S so the result is not too disconcerting. At least they are all there now, so perhaps it was the upside down ones which were missing in Arthur Beckett's day.

Close to the fountain is the aptly named Shepherd and Dog pub, which catered for the 250 humans in the parish in the 19th century. There must have been several dogs as well as shepherds, as there were also two-and-a-half thousand sheep in the area. Now the hostelry doesn't see many shepherds, but plenty of locals and visitors who enjoy the food and drink it offers.

In the days when sheep and shepherding were important in this part of Sussex, many downland villages sent their sheep to be washed in Fulking in May or June before the annual sheep shearing. The clear spring waters here were used for the washing operation, which was carried out by men who stood in the cold water for several hours — not a popular job. The main road was closed to traffic (if there was any) until a man opened a gate at each end to let the few carts pass through. When the washing was done for the day, the men would walk, stiff with cold, to the Shepherd and Dog, to be revived by something a little stronger than water.

After the sheep washing came the shearing, which was normally carried out by a travelling gang. At the completion of this operation, the company would meet at the same inn, to share out their earnings. This meeting was known as The Black Ram.

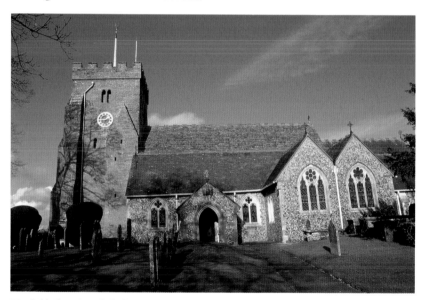

Henfield Church and clock

Fulking and its memory of Ruskin

The sheep-country village of Pycombe lies on the main London to Brighton Road, two and a half miles from Hassocks. Once in East, it is now included in West Sussex. The small church facing the Downs was restored in 1897. It is particularly noted for its rare lead font; rare because there are only two others in Sussex — at Parham and Edburton (and not many more examples in the rest of the country). The lead was cut flat and then bent into shape with just one seam. Tradition says that in the English Civil War the Puritan troops sought out items made of lead and looted the material to make bullets. This could explain why there are so few lead fonts around. But Pycombe folk are wiser than most and they whitewashed their font, so the soldiers missed it.

Pycombe also has another claim to fame, and that is the renowned Pycombe Crook (or more correctly Hook) beloved of old time shepherds. One of the best known of the old Pycombe crook makers was Mr. Berry who worked at the local forge from about 1820 to 1855. It was probably Mr. Berry who originated the particular Pycombe style of hook, although he kept his methods a secret. Experts often say that the best ones were made from old gun barrels. The end of the tool which is known as the guide is curled to avoid becoming a sharp point, and the guide on a Pycombe Crook is longer than on others. Now original examples are highly collectable, and may be seen mainly in museums. Another later blacksmith who made crooks here, was Mr. Charles Mitchell who worked at the forge for around sixty years. He made a pastoral staff for the Bishop of Lewes, which was merely a Pycombe shepherd's crook on a hazel staff.

Devil's Dyke near Poynings is so well known that the legend attached to it scarcely needs re-telling. Briefly it featured the Devil who was always at loggerheads with the obstinate Sussex folk. There are several different variants, but the basis of the tale is that the evil one desired to wipe out all the many little Sussex churches across the Downs and the Weald, and hit upon a plan to wash them away by allowing the sea to pour in through a huge ditch (or Dyke), which he would excavate during one night-time. This he tried, throwing up huge clods of earth which became Chanctonbury and Cissbury Rings, Rackham Hill, Mount Caburn and even the Isle of Wight. A large stone now preserved in Goldstone Park, Hove was also believed to have come from the Devils frantic digging. But as in all the old Sussex legends, the Prince of Darkness was outwitted by the wily country folk, who by various means (the stories differ here), convinced him that dawn had arrived much sooner than it actually had. As he couldn't carry out his evil plan once the night had gone, he was forced to stop digging and is said to have departed to Surrey to have a good sulk. Nearby are two mounds known as the Devil's Grave and the Devil's Wife's Grave. Predictably it is said to be unlucky to walk on them. The Dyke (which is the valley of the Downs, and not the hill as some folk assume), remains as a memorial to devilish plans that miscarried.

The downland village of Pycombe

View at Devil's Dyke on the Downs above Brighton

Although only a tiny Downland village, Clayton has a plethora of famous and interesting features. The railway tunnel dating from 1840 has a most unusual entrance, with a brick-built arch topped with castellated turrets. Behind these a dwelling house was constructed, which must have been extremely noisy and indeed smoky at times. The one-and-a-quarter mile tunnel is particularly noted for the ghastly accident which took place there on a summer Sunday in the August of 1861. Three trains full of day trippers were involved in a pile-up, which resulted in the deaths of 23 passengers, with another 176 people injured. This was the worst railway accident in England to date and must have been particularly unnerving at a time when railways were becoming the most popular form of recreational transport, and the railway builders were congratulating themselves on their great achievements.

The cause of the accident was due to a number of reasons, including mechanical failures, the close proximity of the three trains, and errors by overworked signalmen. No doubt important lessons were learnt, but this was of little consolation to the relatives and friends of those who died. A contemporary account brings the scene graphically alive: "The engine of the third train had literally leaped upon the last carriage of the excursion train, completely smashing it, and then shivering the back of the next carriage into splinters. The two carriages contained sixty persons who were all more or less mutilated, scalded or otherwise injured".

Nearby are the two famous Clayton windmills known affectionately as Jack and Jill. This was often the name for two mills close together, which was not all that unusual at one time in Sussex. Now these two are the only twin mills left in the county. Jack is a brick tower mill built either in 1866 or 1876 — accounts differ. It was erected on the site of an older mill, which was known as Duncton Mill and which dated from 1765. Jill is a wooden post mill of 1821 vintage, which came from Dyke Road, Brighton in about 1850. The moving of the mill must have been a great sight, being carried out initially by a team of horses. Because the horses tended to pull in sharp jerks, the ropes kept breaking, so a team of oxen was substituted and with their slow but steady motive power they succeeded where the horses had failed. This was not the first time a mill had been moved in this fashion, as in 1797 a miller had moved his wooden mill over the Downs, with the help of 86 oxen.

Jill was a working mill until about 1908. Then her fan tackle was damaged and she did not work again. Jack also ceased serious working at about the same time, and shortly afterwards was lived in during the summer months by Edward Martin, a Sussex archaeologist and nature writer. His account of his three years at the mill is affectionately recounted in Life in a Sussex Windmill (1921). When he first moved in he told how "When alone in the place at night , the silences were almost appalling; no other word seems applicable to it."

The tunnel that pretends its a castle

The Sussex twins — Jack and Jill

Ardingly Reservoir was constructed in 1978 when a dam was built across the Southern part of Shell Brook near Ardingly College at a cost of over three million pounds. The capacity of the reservoir is now 5206 megalitres. It is mainly to regulate the water in the river for supply purposes, where water stored above the dam can be released as required into the Ouse. This water augments the flow during dry periods, so that more is available at the Barcombe intake to supply consumers.

The main area of the reservoir is available for recreational uses, such as fishing, sailing, windsurfing and canoeing. It is particularly popular with anglers and members of sailing clubs. There is a public footpath around the peninsula to Balcombe Mill, followed by a bridleway. The Loder Valley Nature Reserve, north of the Causeway is a site of special scientific interest and forms part of the Wakehurst estate, but is not open to the public.

This body of water has a beauty all its own and even before the days of the reservoir it was popular at all times of the year, with many visitors. In previous centuries it was frequently frozen over, sufficiently hard for skating. A diary kept by George Greenfield, estate carpenter at Balcombe Place (1875-1884) has this entry for January 20th 1880. "Went on lake for a stroll. I found it bore me well. Home to tea, after which I took my skates and went and enjoyed myself for an hour upon the lake, home at 8.45pm". In the days following, George continued to amuse himself on the ice, even spending an hour there on Sunday after attending church. He commented "Freezing – great guns".

But not all of George Greenfield's connections with the lake were so enjoyable. In June 1881 he was told that the floodgates were in a bad way. He then took off his shoes and socks and went under the arches of the road to examine the posts. He found trouble, and gave instructions that the water should be drawn down or a sudden influx might cause a serious accident. On September 18th he began work on the flood gates, taking all the old timbers out. In the process he fished out about 14lbs of eels and one fine brown trout. In the days following, George and his men fixed the timber framing of new gates in place and by the end of September the work was done.

Corn was ground at the mill up to the 1920s. In 1801 the miller John Bocker had to provide four sacks of flour a day in the event of a French invasion. The old mill house survives in three sections, all with a tiled roof. The middle part is the original seventeenth century framed house. Local tradition says that milling here went back to Roman times.

Ardingly College, is one of the three Woodward Schools and was opened in 1870. The buildings are in red brick, in the shape of two courtyards. The Chapel was completed in 1883, although without the grandeur of the better known building at Lancing.

The watery expanse of Ardingly reservoir

The old Mill House at Ardingly reservoir

A Sussex Bibliography

As well as the many works I have consulted in writing the text for this book, I have also included other works on Sussex which readers may find of interest.

A

Aitchison, G : Unknown Brighton. 1926
Albery, W : Parliamentary History of Horsham. 1927
A Millenium of Facts in the History of Horsham and Sussex. 1947
Allcroft, A : Downland Pathways. 1924
Allison, F.D : The Little Town of Arundel. 1947
Ambrose, P : The Quiet Revolution. 1974
Armstrong, J.R : A History of Sussex. 1961
Arthur, D : A Sussex Life. 1989
Austen, B : Windmills of Sussex. 1975
Axon, W.E.A : Bygone Sussex. 1897

B

Baker, M.C : Sussex Villages. 1977
Sussex Scenes. 1978
Baldwin, M : The Story of the Forest. 1971
Ballard, A : History of Chichester. 1898
Batten, J : West Sussex Villages. 1982
Beckett, A : The Spirit of the Downs. 1909
The Wonderful Weald. 1911
Adventures of a Quiet Man. 1933
Belloc, H : Sussex. 1906
The Stane Street. 1913
The County of Sussex. 1936
The Four Men.
Blaker, N.P : Sussex in Bygone Days. 1919
Blann, R : A Town's Pride. 1990
Bligh, E : Two Half Moons. 1968
Brabant, F. G : Sussex. 1900
Rambles in Sussex. 1909
Brandon, P : The Sussex Landscape. 1977
The South Saxons. 1978
Brown, L.E : All About Bury. 1948
Brunnarius, M : The Windmills of Sussex. 1979
Budd, M : Dust to Dust. 1966
A Prospect of Love. 1968
Fit for a Duchess. 1970
Burke, J : Sussex. 1974
Burstow, H : Reminicences of Horsham. 1911

C

Candlin, L : Tales of Old Sussex. 1985
Memories of Old Sussex. 1987
Cartland, J : Arundel. A Picture of the Past 1978
Cheal, H : The Story of Shoreham. 1921
Cheal, W.E : Amberley Heritage.
Downland Echoes.
Children of Amberley First School : Secrets of Amberley.
Cooke, A.S : Off the Beaten Track in Sussex.
Colquhoun, E : Around Old and New

Shoreham. 1989
Copper, B : A Song for Every Season. 1971
Songs and Southern Breezes. 1973
Early to Rise. 1976
Across Sussex with Belloc. 1994
Cooper, W.D : A Glossary of Provincialisms in use in the County of Sussex. 1834
Coker-Egerton, J : Sussex Folk and Sussex Ways. New Ed 1892

D

Darby, B : The South Downs. 1976
View of Sussex. 1978
Journey Through the Weald. 1986
Day, A.C : Glimpses of Rural Life in Sussex.
Dickin, J : Chichester Harbour.
Duggan Rees, J : Slindon. A Portrait of a Sussex Village. 1988
The National Trust. Slindon Village.

E

Edwardes, T : Sidelights of Nature in Quill and Crayon. 1898
Lift Luck on Southern Roads. 1910
Neighbourhood. 1911
A Country Calendar. 1928
A Downland Year. 1939
Elleray, D.R : Hastings. A Pictorial History. 1979
The Victorian Churches of Sussex. 1981
Littlehampton. A Pictorial History. 1991
Ellman, E.B : Recollections of a Sussex Parson. 1912
Elphick, G.P : Sussex Bells and Belfries. 1970
Erredge, H : History and Legends of Bramber Castle.
Evans, A. A : On Foot in Sussex. 1933
A Saunterer in Sussex. 1935
By Weald and Down. 1939

F

Fairweather, L : Balcombe. 1981
Fisher, E.A : The Saxon Churches of Sussex. 1970
Fleet, C : Glimpses of our Sussex Ancestors. 1 and 11. 1882/3
Fletcher, A : A County Community in Peace and War. 1975
Francis, M.D : Ancient Arundel. 1921
Fryer, N. Ed : Natural History of St. Leonard's Forest. 1983

G

Garratt, J.G : Bramber and Steyning. 1973
Geering, T : Our Sussex Parish. 1884
Gilbert, E.M : Brighton, Old Ocean's Bauble. 1954
Gill, P and McCann, A : Walks around Historic Chichester. 1980
Goldsworthy, D. Ed : The Sussex Bedside Anthology. 1950

Gosset, A.L.J : Shepherds of Britain. 1911
Gray, J.S : Victorian and Edwardian Brighton in Old Photographs. 1973
Brighton between the Wars. 1976
Green, K : Chichester, Past and Present. 1986
Greenfield, J.A : Tales of Old Petworth. 1976
Gundry, D : Petworth. Today and Yesterday. 1981
Midhurst. Yesterday and Today. 1984

H

Hailsham, J : Idlehurst. 1898
Hannah, I.C : The Sussex Coast. 1912
Hare, A.J.C : Sussex. 1894
Hare, C : Historic Worthing. 1991
Harper, C.G : The Brighton Road. 1892
Harrison, D : Along the South Downs. 1958
Harrison, F and North, J.S : Old Brighton, Old Hove, Old Preston. 1937
Hayman, R : The First Thrust. 1975
Hickman, M.M : The History of Shipley 1947
Holman, G : Sussex in the Past. 1930
Hopkins, T : Kipling's Sussex. 1921
Sheila Kaye-Smith and the Weald country. 1925
Sussex Pilgrimages. 1927
The Lure of Sussex. 1928
Kipling's Sussex Revisited. 1929
A Detective in Sussex. 1932
The Man who was Sussex. 1933
Literary Originals of Sussex. 1936
Sussex Rendezvous.
Horsfield, T.W : The History, Antiquities and Topography of the County of Sussex. 1835
Hudson, T.P : Victoria History of Sussex.
Husdon, W.H : Nature in Downland. 1900
Hurst, Lady D : Horsham. Its History and Antiquities. 1868

I

Itchenor-Church and Village.

J

Jennett, S : South Downs Way. 1977
Jennings, L.J : Field Paths and Green Lanes in Surrey and Sussex. 1877
Jerrome, P : Cloakbag and Common Purse. 1979
Jerrome, P and Newdick, J : Not Submitted Elsewhere. 1980
Proud Petworth and Beyond. 1981
Petworth. Time out of Mind. 1982
Petworth. The Winds of Change.
Men with Laughter in their Hearts. 1986
Old and New. Teasing and True. 1988
Johnson, W : Talks with Shepherds. 1925

K

Kaye-Smith, S : The Weald of Kent and Sussex. 1953

Kenyon, H : Kirdford. Some Parish History. 1971
Kipling, R : Puck of Pook's Hill. 1906
Reward and Fairies. 1910

L

Latham, C : Some West Sussex Superstitions Lingering in 1868.
Leigh, L : The Roadmender Country. 1922
Leigh, R : Past and Passing. 1932
Lower, M.A : Contributions to Literature. 1854
Lowerson, J : A Short History of Sussex. 1980
Lowerson, J and Myerscough, J : Time to Spare in Victorian England. 1977
Lucas, E.V : Highways and Byways in Sussex. 1904

M

Mais, S.P.B : Hills of the South. 1939
The Land of the Cinque Ports. 1949
Sussex. 1950
Manxse, Lady : Petworth in Ancient Times. 1952
Martin, E.A : Life in a Sussex Windmill. 1921
Massingham, H.J : English Downland. 1936
Maxwell, D : Unknown Sussex. 1923
A Detective in Sussex. 1932
McDermott, R and R : The Standing Windmills of West Sussex. 1978
McEwan, S : Clayton Windmills. ND
Mee, A : The Kings England. Sussex. 1937
Meynell, E : Sussex Cottage. 1936
Country Ways. 1942
Cottage Tale. 1946
Small Talk in Sussex. 1954
Sussex.
Migod, F.W.H : Worthing. A Survey of Times Past and Present. 1938
Montgomery, J : History, People and Places in West Sussex. 1977

N

Nairn, I and Pevsner, N : The Buildings of England. Sussex. 1965

O

Ogley, B, Currie, I and Davison, M : The Sussex Weather Book. 1991

P

Pailthorpe, R and Serraillier, I : Goodwood Country in Old Photographs. 1987
Parish, Rev. W.D : Dictionary of the Sussex Dialect. 1875
Payne, S and Pailthorpe, R : The Downland Shepherds. 1989
Phillips, W.W.A and Kraunsoe, L : The Natural History of Pagham Harbour. Part

1. 1979
Price, B : Bygone Chichester. 1975
Sussex. People, Places, Things. 1975

R

Rayner, R.W.Ed : The Natural History of Pagham Harbour. Part 2 1981
Rees, A.J : Old Sussex and her Diarists. 1929
Robinson, M : A South Down Farm in the Sixties. 1938
Roundell, Mrs C : Cowdray. The History of a Great English House. 1884
Rudkin, M.S : Seeing Sussex. 1930

S

Scott, H : Secret Sussex. 1949
Secretan, D.L : Balcombe. 1937
Simpson, J : The Folklore of Sussex. 1973
Smail, H : Coaching Times and After. 1948
The Worthing Map Story. 1949
Staines, E.N : Dear Amberley. 1968
Straker, E : Wealden Iron. 1931
Sweatman, W.F, Wharton, W.A, and Durrant, W.H : The Story of Thakeham Meeting House and the Blue Idol Guest House. 1961
Swinfen, W and Arscott, D : Hidden Sussex. 1984
People of Hidden Sussex. 1985
Hidden Sussex Day by Day. 1987
Hidden Sussex - The Towns. 1990

T

Taylor, J : The Sussex Garland.. 1851
Taylor, R : The East Sussex Village Book. 1986
Sussex Scandals. 1987
Tiltman, M.H : Cottage Pie. 1940
A Little Place in the Country. 1944
The Birds Began to Sing. 1952
Turner, J.T : The London, Brighton and South Coast Railway. 3 Volumes. 1977-9
Turner, T : Diary. Ed by D Vaisey. 1884
Thompson, H.J.F : Littlehampton Long Ago. 1974
Littlehampton Through the Wars. 1978
The Swing Bridge Story. 1979
The Picturemakers. 1981

V

Vine, J.E : London's Lost Route to the Sea. 1965

W

Wales, T : We Wunt be Druv. 1976
A Sussex Garland. 1979
A Day Out in Old Sussex. 1982
Long Summer Days. 1983
The West Sussex Village Book. 1984
Horsham in Old Picture Postcards, Volume 1. 1987

Ballads, Bands and Bellringers. 1989
An Album of Old Horsham. 1989
Sussex Customs, Curiosities and Country Lore. 1990
Horsham in Old Picture Postcards, Volume 2. 1992
Sussex Ghosts and Legends. 1992
Littlehampton in Old Picture Postcards. 1993
Fabulous Horsham.
Wales, T and Green, A. E. Ed : Henry Burstow's Reminiscences of Horsham. 1975
Waugh, M : Smuggling in Kent and Sussex. 1985
White, S : Around Worthing in Old Photographs. 1991
W. I : West Sussex Within Living Memory. 1983
Wills, B : Bypaths in Downland. 1927
Downland Treasure. 1929
Shepherds of Sussex.
Winbolt, S.E : With a Spade on Stane Street. 1936
Winbolt, S.E and Herbert, G : The Roman Villa at Bignor Sussex. 1925
Windrum, A : Horsham. An Historical Survey. 1978
Windrum, A and Hughes, A : Bygone Horsham. 1982
Wood, F.E : Round About a Sussex Village. 1921
Round About Sussex Downs. 1925
Sport and Nature in Sussex Downs. 1928
Wood, W : A Sussex Farmer. 1938
Woodforde, C : Portrait of Sussex. 1975
Woodman, T.C : The Geology of Sussex. 1899
The South Downs. 1901
Woodward, M : Mistress of Stantons Farm. 1938
Wolseley, Viscountess : The Countrymans Log Book. 1921
Sussex in the Past 1928
Some Sussex Byways. 1930
Myth and Memory. 1934
Wymer, N : Companion into Sussex. 1972

Y

Young, G : The Cottage in the Fields. 1945
The Chronicle of a Country Cottage.
Come into the Country.
Down Hoe Lane. 1950
A History of Bognor Regis. 1983

Acknowledgements also to many local guide books, Sussex newspapers, Southern Water Board, South East Water and Mr R. Godliman for information on the Ardingly Reservoir.